William Shakespeare's

JULIUS CAESAR

NOTES

Edited and with an Introduction by
HAROLD BLOOM

First Printing
1 3 5 7 9 8 6 4 2

ISBN: 0-7910-3680-4

Chelsea House Publishers
1974 Sproul Road, Suite 400
P.O. Box 914
Broomall, PA 19008-0914

Contents

User's Guide

This volume is designed to present biographical, critical, and bibliographical information on William Shakespeare and *Julius Caesar*. Following Harold Bloom's introduction, there appears a detailed biography of the author, discussing the major events in his life and his important literary works. Then follows a thematic and structural analysis of the work, in which significant themes, patterns, and motifs are traced. An annotated list of characters supplies brief information on the chief characters in the work.

A selection of critical extracts, derived from previously published material by leading critics, then follows. The extracts consist of such things as statements by the author on his work, early reviews of the work, and later evaluations down to the present day. The items are arranged chronologically by date of first publication. A bibliography of Shakespeare's writings (including a complete listing of all the books he wrote, cowrote, edited, and translated in his lifetime, and important posthumous publications), a list of additional books and articles on him and on *Julius Caesar*, and an index of themes conclude the volume.

Harold Bloom is Sterling Professor of the Humanities at Yale University and Henry W. and Albert A. Berg Professor of English at the New York University Graduate School. He is the author of twenty books and the editor of more than thirty anthologies of literature and literary criticism.

Professor Bloom's works include *Shelley's Mythmaking* (1959), *The Visionary Company* (1961), *Blake's Apocalypse* (1963), *Yeats* (1970), *A Map of Misreading* (1975), *Kabbalah and Criticism* (1975), and *Agon: Towards a Theory of Revisionism* (1982). *The Anxiety of Influence* (1973) sets forth Professor Bloom's provocative theory of the literary relationships between the great writers and their predecessors. His most recent books are *The American Religion* (1992) and *The Western Canon* (1994).

Professor Bloom earned his Ph.D. from Yale University in 1955 and has served on the Yale faculty since then. He is a 1985 MacArthur Foundation Award recipient and served as the Charles Eliot Norton Professor of Poetry at Harvard University in 1987–88. He is currently the editor of the Chelsea House series Major Literary Characters and Modern Critical Views, and other Chelsea House series in literary criti-

Introduction

HAROLD BLOOM

Shakespeare's *Julius Caesar,* though in some respects it is almost the model of a "well-made play," is nevertheless a remarkably ambiguous work. Julius Caesar himself is at the center of the ambiguity: how does Shakespeare's drama wish us to regard Caesar? By the time he composed *Antony and Cleopatra,* Shakespeare's mastery of perspectivism had so increased that we tend hardly to notice that the ambiguities also had vastly heightened. Whether you regard Cleopatra as a protogoddess, a whore, or something in between, is likely to say more about you than about the role that Shakespeare created. But in *Julius Caesar,* your attitude towards Caesar might only indicate your politics, since everything in Shakespeare's representation of the Roman hero (even that word is problematical) is capable of multiple interpretations. Beyond question, Caesar is Shakespeare's only historical character of worldwide importance (unless you count the Octavius of *Antony and Cleopatra,* who has not yet become the first emperor of Rome, Augustus Caesar). Shakespeare wrote no play about Alexander the Great; Julius Caesar is a comparable figure, which makes Shakespeare's treatment of him all the more surprising, even disconcerting.

Despite the play's title, Caesar's is only a supporting role in what should be called *The Tragedy of Marcus Brutus.* Caesar, after all, is on stage for only three scenes, is dead before the halfway point, and speaks perhaps one hundred and forty lines. And yet he is the atmosphere of the play, its world, almost its nature despite the uneven quality of his speeches, which vary from an egotistic inanity to a noble, virtually godlike intensity of being. Some critics have suggested that the Julius Caesar of Shakespeare is cunningly less interested in an earthly crown than he is in his metamorphosis into a god. He already rules Rome; all that he can gain by provoking the conspirators is a martyr's death that ensures his status as a god and that guarantees the Roman Empire that will be inaugurated by his nephew Octavius Caesar. In a strange sense, Caesar seems to have chosen the risk of being slain as a sacrifice to his own greatness. Brutus, who has enjoyed a son's relationship to Caesar, urges his fellow assassins to carve up the dictator as a sacrifice fit for the gods, a sentiment by which the Stoic Brutus intends no irony, though Shakespeare's own irony is evident, as it is throughout much of the play.

Brutus, as the drama's protagonist, is himself presented with considerable ambiguity, perhaps because he is an anticipation of Hamlet, prince of ambiguities. Self-righteous and morally rather vain, Brutus takes for granted his own disinterestedness, a dangerous assumption in this most political of Shakespeare's plays, with the possible exception of the later *Coriolanus*. I think, *contra* Freud, that there is Oedipal conflict in Hamlet, but there certainly is one in Brutus, as there will be in Macbeth. Brutus cannot understand his own ambivalences towards Caesar and is thus unable to ward off the influence of Cassius, who knows very well why he resents Caesar. The relation between Brutus and Cassius seems to me the subtlest in the play and the most dramatic. Cassius's love for Brutus is a veneration that he denies to Caesar and that Brutus scarcely reciprocates, because Brutus is indeed so powerfully self-centered. That Brutus is noble and stoical is not to be denied, but Shakespeare has endowed this Roman hero with considerable narcissism. As a Stoic, Brutus is able to divide his reason and his passions from one another, yet Shakespeare may have made Brutus too much of a Stoic to be able to move us as profoundly as we are moved by the protagonists of the other tragedies. Since Brutus demonstrates a constant, highly conscious self-control, we have some difficulty at seeing into the abyss of his self. Yet Shakespeare provides us with enough representation of division in Brutus's soul so as to render him a tragic figure, flawed in judgment and hemmed in by his absolute conviction of his own virtue. He is so identified with his own vision of Rome that he simply does not know where he ends and where Rome begins. Though Cassius draws him into the plot to murder Caesar, he offers virtually no resistance and sees himself as fated to sacrifice Caesar to the gods. As leader of the assassins, Brutus is not less than a disaster. Cassius urges, sensibly, that Mark Antony be slain with Caesar; Brutus refuses, and yet events prove Cassius to have been correct. Again, Cassius shrewdly seeks to deny Antony the chance of a funeral oration for Caesar; Brutus overrules Cassius, with dark results for the conspirators. Finally, Brutus insists upon marching to Philippi for the final battle, and again Cassius yields out of affection and so forfeits his better judgment.

In his death speech, Brutus moves us when he rejoices that "in all my life / I found no man but he was true to me." But then we reflect that Brutus, of all the conspirators, was most untrue to Caesar, who loved him. This irony, to which Brutus is blind, marks his limits once more. And yet, there is indeed a premonition of Hamlet's greatness in Brutus: the Roman hero's meditations presage the grand speculations of Shakespeare's principal intellectual. Against the charismatic consciousness of Brutus, Shakespeare sets the nature of the political failure, perhaps even political crime: to murder Julius Caesar is to strike against the entire tradition of kingship that descends from Caesar, a tradition that includes, however remotely, Queen Elizabeth I herself. Shakespeare is both subtle and careful in the balance of this tragedy: Brutus is the tragic hero, but his identification with Rome is more flaw than virtue, and it destroys him. ✤

Biography of William Shakespeare

Few events in the life of William Shakespeare are supported by reliable evidence, and many incidents recorded by commentators of the last four centuries are either conjectural or apocryphal.

William Shakespeare was born in Stratford-upon-Avon on April 22 or 23, 1564, the son of Mary Arden and John Shakespeare, a tradesman. His very early education was in the hands of a tutor, for his parents were probably illiterate. At age seven he entered the Free School in Stratford, where he learned the "small Latin and less Greek" attributed to him by Ben Jonson. When not in school Shakespeare may have gone to the popular Stratford fairs and to the dramas and mystery plays performed by traveling actors.

When Shakespeare was about thirteen his father removed him from school and apprenticed him to a butcher, although it is not known how long he remained in this occupation. When he was eighteen he married Anne Hathaway; their first child, Susanna, was born six months later. A pair of twins, Hamnet and Judith, were born in February 1585. About this time Shakespeare was caught poaching deer on the estate of Sir Thomas Lucy of Charlecot; Lucy's prosecution is said to have inspired Shakespeare to write his earliest literary work, a satire on his opponent. Shakespeare was convicted of poaching and forced to leave Stratford. He withdrew to London, leaving his family behind. He soon attached himself to the stage, initially in a menial capacity (as tender of playgoers' horses, according to one tradition), then as prompter's attendant. When the poaching furor subsided, Shakespeare returned to Stratford to join one of the many bands of itinerant actors. In the next five years he gained what little theatre training he received.

By 1592 Shakespeare was a recognized actor, and in that year he wrote and produced his first play, *Henry the Sixth, Part One.* Its success impelled Shakespeare soon afterward to write the second and third parts of *Henry the Sixth.* (Many early and modern critics believed that *Love's Labour's Lost* preceded these histories as Shakespeare's earliest play, but the majority of modern scholars discount this theory.) Shakespeare's popularity provoked the jealousy of Robert Greene, as recorded in his posthumous *Groats-worth of Wit* (1592).

In 1593 Shakespeare published *Venus and Adonis,* a long poem based upon Ovid (or perhaps upon Arthur Golding's translation of Ovid's *Metamorphoses*). It was dedicated to the young Earl of Southampton—but perhaps without permission, a possible indication that Shakespeare was trying to gain the nobleman's patronage. However, the dedicatory address to Southampton in the poem *The Rape of Lucrece* (1594) reveals Shakespeare to have been on good terms with him. Many plays—such as *Titus Andronicus, The Comedy of Errors,* and *Romeo and Juliet*—were produced over the next several years, most performed by Shakespeare's troupe, the Lord Chamberlain's Company. In December 1594 Shakespeare acted in a comedy (of unknown authorship) before Queen Elizabeth; many other royal performances followed in the next decade.

In August 1596 Shakespeare's son Hamnet died. Early the next year Shakespeare bought a home, New Place, in the center of Stratford; he is said to have planted a mulberry tree in the backyard with his own hands. Shakespeare's relative prosperity is indicated by his purchasing more than a hundred acres of farmland in 1602, a cottage near his estate later that year, and half-interest in the tithes of some local villages in 1605.

In September 1598 Shakespeare began his friendship with the then unknown Ben Jonson by producing his play *Every Man in His Humour.* The next year the publisher William Jaggard affixed Shakespeare's name, without his permission, to a curious medley of poems under the title *The Passionate Pilgrim;* the majority of the poems were not by Shakespeare. Two of his sonnets, however, appeared in this collection, although the 154 sonnets, with their mysterious dedication to "Mr. W. H.," were not published as a group until 1609. Also in 1599 the Globe Theatre was built in Southwark (an area of London), and Shakespeare's company began acting there. Many of his greatest plays—*Troilus and Cressida, King Lear, Othello, Macbeth*—

were performed in the Globe before its destruction by fire in 1613.

The death in 1603 of Queen Elizabeth, the last of the Tudors, and the accession of James I, from the Stuart dynasty of Scotland, created anxiety throughout England. Shakespeare's fortunes, however, were unaffected, as the new monarch extended the license of Shakespeare's company to perform at the Globe. James I saw a performance of *Othello* at the court in November 1604. In October 1605 Shakespeare's company performed before the Mayor and Corporation of Oxford.

The last five years of Shakespeare's life seem void of incident; he had retired from the stage by 1613. Among the few known incidents is Shakespeare's involvement in a heated and lengthy dispute about the enclosure of common-fields around Stratford. He died on April 23, 1616, and was buried in the Church of St. Mary's in Stratford. A monument was later erected to him in the Poets' Corner of Westminster Abbey.

Numerous corrupt quarto editions of Shakespeare's plays were published during his lifetime. These editions, based either on manuscripts, promptbooks, or sometimes merely actors' recollections of the plays, were meant to capitalize on Shakespeare's renown. Other plays, now deemed wholly or largely spurious—*Edward the Third, The Yorkshire Tragedy, The Two Noble Kinsmen,* and others—were also published under Shakespeare's name during and after his lifetime. Shakespeare's plays were collected in the First Folio of 1623 by John Heminge and Henry Condell. Nine years later the Second Folio was published, and in 1640 Shakespeare's poems were collected. The first standard collected edition was by Nicholas Rowe (1709), followed by the editions of Alexander Pope (1725), Lewis Theobald (1733), Samuel Johnson (1765), Edmond Malone (1790), and many others.

Shakespeare's plays are now customarily divided into the following categories (probable dates of writing are given in brackets): comedies (*The Comedy of Errors* [1590], *The Taming of the Shrew* [1592], *The Two Gentlemen of Verona* [1592–93], *A Midsummer Night's Dream* [1595], *Love's Labour's Lost* [1595], *The Merchant of Venice* [1596–98], *As You Like It*

[1597], *The Merry Wives of Windsor* [1597], *Much Ado About Nothing* [1598–99], *Twelfth Night* [1601], *All's Well That Ends Well* [1603–04], and *Measure for Measure* [1604]); histories (*Henry the Sixth, Part One* [1590–92], *Henry the Sixth, Parts Two and Three* [1590–92], *Richard the Third* [1591], *King John* [1591–98], *Richard the Second* [1595], *Henry the Fourth, Part One* [1597], *Henry the Fourth, Part Two* [1597], *Henry the Fifth* [1599], and *Henry the Eighth* [1613]); tragedies (*Titus Andronicus* [1590], *Romeo and Juliet* [1595], *Julius Caesar* [1599], *Hamlet* [1599–1601], *Troilus and Cressida* [1602], *Othello* [1602–04], *King Lear* [1604–05], *Macbeth* [1606], *Timon of Athens* [1607], *Antony and Cleopatra* [1606–07], and *Coriolanus* [1608]); romances (*Pericles, Prince of Tyre* [1606–08], *Cymbeline* [1609–10], *The Winter's Tale* [1610–11], and *The Tempest* [1611]). However, Shakespeare willfully defied the canons of classical drama by mingling comedy, tragedy, and history, so that in some cases classification is debatable or arbitrary.

Shakespeare's reputation, while subject to many fluctuations, was firmly established by the eighteenth century. Samuel Johnson remarked: "Perhaps it would not be easy to find any authour, except Homer, who invented so much as Shakespeare, who so much advanced the studies which he cultivated, who effused so much novelty upon his age or country. The form, the characters, the language, and the shows of the English drama are his." Early in the nineteenth century Samuel Taylor Coleridge declared: "The Englishman who without reverence, a proud and affectionate reverence, can utter the name of William Shakespeare, stands disqualified for the office of critic. . . . Great as was the genius of Shakespeare, his judgment was at least equal to it."

A curious controversy developed in the middle of the nineteenth century in regard to the authorship of Shakespeare's plays, some contending that Sir Francis Bacon was the actual author of the plays, others (including Mark Twain) advancing the claims of the Earl of Oxford. None of these attempts has succeeded in persuading the majority of scholars that Shakespeare himself is not the author of the plays attributed to him.

In recent years many landmark editions of Shakespeare, with increasingly accurate texts and astute critical commentary, have emerged. These include the New Cambridge Shakespeare (1921–62) and the New Arden Shakespeare (1951f.). Such critics as T. S. Eliot, G. Wilson Knight, Northrop Frye, W. H. Auden, and many others have continued to elucidate Shakespeare, his work, and his times, and he remains the most written-about author in the history of English literature. ❖

Thematic and Structural Analysis

The representation of human personality in its full depth and complexity is perhaps the highest task of literature. No writer has performed this task as magnificently as Shakespeare. In his greatest plays, such as *Hamlet, Macbeth, Othello,* or *King Lear,* Shakespeare captures the manifold thoughts, passions, impulses, dilemmas, doubts, drives, quirks, and conflicts of human selfhood with a subtlety and sharpness that have seldom been rivaled. *Julius Caesar* does not belong among these greatest of Shakespeare's dramas. It was written early in his career, and it is shorter, less assured, and less ambitious than the monumental works of his full maturity. It is nonetheless significant as an early foray toward the depths of soul that he would later plumb more thoroughly. With the complicated but relatively undeveloped characters of Brutus and Mark Antony at its heart, *Julius Caesar* can be read in part as a sketch—a preparatory drawing of the kinds of figures that are later more fully rendered in *Hamlet, Richard III,* or *Othello.*

More fully, *Julius Caesar* must be read as a play about politics. Its plot centers on the political assassination of a great general, and thematically it takes up the time-honored question as to which is the best regime—in this case, either monarchy or democracy. But in keeping with his primary interest in human personality, Shakespeare places these political issues in a richly psychological context. *Julius Caesar* ultimately says little by way of a positive theoretical defense of democracy over monarchy or vice versa; but it says a great deal about the feelings elicited by these different types of political order. Like his own beloved Queen Elizabeth, for example, Shakespeare's Julius Caesar is impressive in his ability to inspire in people a passionate sense of admiration and reverence. Such a charismatic figure, however, inevitably arouses bitter envy and resentment among powerful rivals, in this case Cassius and his co-conspirators. Republican or democratic ideals, on the other hand, are capable of appealing to what one might call the passion of equality—the deep-rooted feeling, so eloquently articulated by Cassius in Act I, that no one is inherently superior to oneself. The people en masse are also emotionally fickle, however, and are therefore easy prey to the kind of brilliant rhetorical arts practiced by Mark Antony in Act III, scene 1. Shakespeare's interest in politics is thus intimately connected to his interest in human personality. Both, for him, are primarily matters of feeling.

The theme of shifting political passions is raised immediately as the play begins. In **Act I, scene 1,** Marullus and Flavius encounter a crowd of commoners gathering in the street in anticipation of Julius Caesar's return from his victorious battle against Pompey in the Roman civil war. The two tribunes banter with the people, scolding them for the shortness of their memory of Pompey, the former first citizen, whom once they loved. "O you hard hearts," Marullus says, "you cruel men of Rome,/ Knew you not Pompey?" Marullus and Flavius then go to remove the ornaments from the statues that have been recently put up in honor of Caesar.

Caesar himself takes the stage in **Act I, scene 2.** The effect at first is one of emerging power and authority, as Caesar and his retinue proceed through the streets amidst fawning crowds. Shakespeare quickly moves the focus inward, however, and reveals some of the vanity and presumptuousness beneath Caesar's show of confidence. It is the day of the feast of the Lupercalia, a fertility rite held in honor of the legendary she-wolf who suckled Rome's founders when they were children. Two naked young noblemen traditionally run a race through the city during this feast, playfully striking with a thong any woman they come across. The thong is believed to confer fertility on those who are touched by it. Caesar is seen urging his wife, Calphurnia, who is as yet childless, to stand in the path of Mark Antony as he runs the race. The implication is that Caesar already expects to be made a king, and he is eager for his wife to bear him a son who might inherit his title. This expectation of royal succession runs directly counter to the Republican principles that at this point still govern Rome. When a soothsayer emerges from the crowd and three times warns Caesar to "Beware the ides of march" (March 15, the following day), the audience begins to suspect that the brash warrior may be in the process of overstepping his bounds.

Caesar and his retinue presently exit, leaving the eminent noblemen Cassius and Brutus alone on stage. Cassius, we soon discover, is intensely resentful of the power and adulation being showered on Caesar, and he has already resolved, along with several friends, to attempt to assassinate the victorious general. He wishes to enlist Brutus' aid in the plot, hoping that Brutus' reputation for virtue and wisdom will lend moral weight to the cause. A conversation ensues in which Cassius attempts to draw his friend out by asking him why he has been distant and preoccupied recently. Brutus initially deflects Cassius' inquiries, saying he is distracted by personal matters. But Cassius persists, reminding Brutus that he is greatly admired by the nobles as well as by the common people and cautiously suggesting that in the near future he may be called upon to take up a special public duty. Brutus does not respond to Cassius' hint, noting instead the shouts going up on a nearby street and commenting that he fears the people are choosing Caesar for king. Cassius leaps at the opening provided by this remark, saying that if Brutus *fears* this result, that means he must not *desire* it. Brutus assents to Cassius' conclusion, but reminds him that he still loves Caesar. At this point Cassius launches into a long and moving speech, expressing passionately democratic convictions. Cassius tells Brutus the story of how he once had to save Caesar when they attempted to swim together across the stormy Tiber, and of how when Caesar was sick with a fever he groaned and cried for help like any other man. "I was born as free as Caesar," Cassius declaims, "so were you: / We both have fed as well, and we can both / Endure the winter's cold as well as he . . . / . . . and this man / Is now become a god, and Cassius is / a wretched creature, and must bend his body / If Caesar carelessly but nod on him." Cassius' eloquence strikes a spark in the prudent and reserved Brutus. He will not directly or explicitly agree to participate in Cassius' designs, but he does promise to give the matter serious consideration.

The need for such reflection is further emphasized in the latter part of **Act I, scene 2,** when Casca informs Brutus and Cassius that Flavius and Marullus have been "silenced" for removing the ornaments from Caesar's statues, and that the crowd has indeed offered a crown to Caesar three times.

Although Caesar rejected it all three times, Casca tells them, he did so with increasingly visible reluctance. And the crowd was only made all the more worshipful by Caesar's pretended diffidence. As they disperse, Cassius delivers a brief soliloquy in which he informs the audience of his intention to draw Brutus further into his schemes by throwing messages attached to stones through the esteemed nobleman's window that evening. He will write out the messages in different hands, he tells us, so that Brutus will think that many Romans want him to take action. It says much about Brutus' virtuousness that Cassius knows that the best way to manipulate him is to make him believe he is acting in the interests of society as a whole. It says much about Cassius' ruthlessness that he is willing to deceive his dearest friend for the sake of his obsessive cause. We see him in active pursuit of that cause in the next and final scene of Act I (**I.3**). He moves about the city on a storm-torn night, meeting secretly with his co-conspirators. He interprets the wild weather and other portents as signs of the cosmic disorder caused by Caesar's overreaching, and he swears he will kill himself rather than submit to the authority of a Roman king.

In **Act II** the focus shifts away from Cassius to Brutus and Caesar himself. We first find Brutus alone in his orchard very late on the same stormy night that concluded Act I. In meditating on the question of whether to join in Cassius' plot against Caesar, Brutus places a psychological question uppermost. It is clear to him that Caesar wants to be king. It is unclear, however, if this would be good for Rome. He himself has nothing personal against Caesar. Indeed, Brutus believes that Caesar has always wielded his power as a military leader in a humane and responsible manner. But the question that cannot be answered is whether Caesar would continue to behave so justly once he was granted the tremendous authority of kingship. Brutus puts the problem to himself vividly and eloquently:

> He would be crowned.
> How that might change his nature, there's the question.
> It is the bright day that brings forth the adder,
> And that craves wary walking. Crown him that,
> And then I grant we put a sting in him
> That at his will he may do danger with.

Th' abuse of greatness is when it disjoins
Remorse from power. . . .

Brutus here thinks about politics in the same way that we have said Shakespeare does throughout the play—in terms of feeling. To "disjoin remorse from power" is not to adopt an erroneous political theory; it is to become cold and heartless in the process of exercising authority, and thus to become dehumanized. As Brutus reflects further, he becomes convinced that human nature is such that power would inevitably change Caesar's personality in this way, and that therefore he must be prevented from gaining kingship. A letter brought to Brutus by his servant, which incites the senator to action against Caesar on behalf of all Romans, confirms his resolution.

When Cassius and the conspirators arrive later, in the small hours of the morning, Brutus promises his full cooperation. In keeping with his noble and gentle nature, however, he will not allow them to swear an oath on their pact, insisting that for true Romans a promise must suffice. And he will not allow them to extend the plot to include an attack on Mark Antony, Caesar's close friend and ally. "Let's be sacrificers, but not butchers," he says. "Let's carve him as a dish fit for the gods, / Not hew him as a carcass fit for hounds." Even in such a bloody deed, Brutus insists, they must maintain a proper emotional balance: "And let our hearts, as subtle masters do, / Stir up their servants to an act of rage / And after seem to chide 'em." The other conspirators agree to Brutus' stipulations and depart. Portia, Brutus' wife, then enters and pleads with Brutus to tell her what his visitors wanted. A wife should be told, she insists, about whatever cares weigh so heavily on her husband that they keep him from sleeping. Brutus avoids her questioning, however, and the scene ends as Ligarius arrives and pledges himself to the conspiracy.

In the next scene (**II.2**) it is Caesar who is up from his bed, in nightclothes. He has been awakened by his wife, Calphurnia, who three times cried out in her dreams, "Help, ho! They murder Caesar!" Although he is famous for mocking the pretensions of Roman soothsayers in his book on the Gallic Wars, he is now sufficiently alarmed that he sends his servant to tell the priests to make sacrifices and to inform him of their opinion of his chances for success. His defiance returns, however, when Calphurnia awakens and advises him to stay safely inside for the day. She tells him of the many dismal portents seen by the nightwatchman, including graves opening and ghosts "shrieking and squealing about the streets." But Caesar's only response is a sturdy Stoic fatalism. "What can be avoided," he asks calmly, "whose end is purposed by the mighty gods?" He continues to insist on going before the Senate that day even after the servant returns to tell him that the augurers urge him not to stir forth. It is only Calphurnia's repeated pleas that finally sway him. Caesar finally gives in to her repeated warnings and decides to inform the Senate that he does not wish to appear this day. No sooner has he come to this conclusion, however, than the conspirator Decius arrives and succeeds in changing his mind. He makes Caesar believe he will be laughed at if he tells the Senate he is sick. And, more importantly, Decius reinterprets Calphurnia's dream in a light favorable to the general. In her dream, Calphurnia had seen a statue of Caesar running with blood from "a hundred spouts." Whereas Calphurnia had read this symbol to suggest Caesar's death by stabbing, Decius cleverly glosses it as "a vision fair and fortunate." The Romans bathing in Caesar's blood, Decius suggests, really signifies the revival of Rome by means of Caesar's life-giving force. Decius says he knows this is the appropriate interpretation, furthermore, because he knows that the Senate intends this day to offer Caesar the crown. If he fails to appear for such an occasion, Decius urges, it could be taken as a gesture of scorn for the Senate or, worse, as a sign of fear, and the senators might then change their minds. Caesar is convinced by Decius' arguments and sets off with him for the Senate, regretting that he ever allowed Calphurnia's fears to affect him. The irony is that the general who was famous for ignoring the advice of fortune-tellers is here forced to choose between two interpretations of a portentous image from a dream. Unfortunately for him, he makes the wrong choice.

The second act ends with two short scenes. The first (**II.3**) consists only of a character by the name of Artemidorus reading aloud from a sheet of paper on a street near the capitol. His reading is a blunt warning to Caesar to beware of precisely those noblemen whom we have seen plotting against him. Artemidorus announces his intention to position himself on the side of the street near where Caesar will pass on his way to the Senate and to give him this message. He articulates one of the central tragic themes of the play when he says, "My heart laments that virtue cannot live / Out of the teeth of emulation." (Emulation, in Elizabethan English, implied envious rivalry, rather than benign imitation of virtuous models.) In **Act II, scene 4** we see the almost frantic anxiety of Portia as she waits at home after Brutus has gone to the Senate building. It becomes clear that Brutus has informed her of the plot against Caesar, and she is nearly beside herself with desire for news of what has transpired. She manages to suppress ber urges to tell someone what she knows, but she does send a servant to Brutus with the apparently inane message that she is "merry." Presumably any message would suffice; she merely wants the servant to go to the Senate building to find out what has happened.

What has happened (**Act III, scene 1**) is exactly what Cassius had long hoped would happen. Under the pretext of appealing for Caesar's permission to allow a banished citizen to return, the conspirators gather closely around the proud warrior and stab him to death. The pathos of the moment is famously captured by Caesar's dying words as Brutus adds his knife to the rest. "Et tu, Brute?" ("Even you, Brutus?") he asks, expressing an almost gentle surprise that a man with Brutus' exalted reputation for probity and fair-mindedness should have involved himself in such a base scheme. The simple three-word question opens up again the whole agonizing issue of whether or not Brutus has acted justly. There is no time left now, however, for Brutus to return to the introspective mood of the first two acts. He and his allies bathe their hands in Caesar's blood as a sign of their continued unity and turn their attention to what today we would call "spin control"—publicizing the event in the most favorable light possible. Worried about a backlash against the killers of the popular leader, Cassius sends some of the band out to "the common pulpits" to announce that the deed was done in the service of "Liberty, Freedom, Enfranchisement!" The rest are about to set out toward the Forum with the same message when a servant of Mark Antony enters. He offers

Mark Antony's loyalty to Brutus, saying he loved Caesar, but that he will love Brutus more if peace can be established between them. Brutus accepts the offer with characteristic graciousness, and Antony himself soon enters. The exchange that follows is the first demonstration of Antony's immense capacity for duplicity. He shakes the bloody hands of each of the assassins, at the same time eloquently lamenting the death of his leader—"the choice and master spirit of the age." More importantly, he manages to convince Brutus to allow him to speak at Caesar's funeral, claiming he only wishes to honor publicly a leader he loved. Cassius suspects that Antony will use the occasion to stir up the populace against the assassins, but Brutus reassures Cassius, saying he will also speak himself and make clear the righteousness of their action. The scene ends with a passionate soliloquy by Mark Antony, vowing "woe to the hand that shed this costly blood!" "A curse shall light upon the limbs of men," he proclaims, "Domestic fury and fierce civil strife / Shall cumber all the parts of Italy." Upon concluding, he dispatches a servant to Caesar's brother-in-law Octavius, warning him not to enter the city until he has tested the mood of the people at Caesar's funeral.

The following scene (**Act III, scene 2**) is one of the most famous in all Shakespeare. Brutus and Mark Antony take the pulpit by turns and address the crowd that has gathered for Caesar's funeral. First Brutus explains that he loved Caesar as much as any man, but that he loves Rome more. He killed Caesar in order to protect Rome and Romans from the tryranny that would have resulted from Caesar's insatiable ambition. The plebeian crowd is deeply swayed by Brutus' eloquent words. As Brutus descends from the pulpit, they clamor in affirmation of what he has said, praising his courage and nobility, and agreeing that Caesar was a tyrant. This view of things does not last very long, however. Following Brutus, Mark Antony takes the pulpit and with consummate verbal artistry manages to undermine everything Brutus has said. He cites Caesar's rejection of the crown as evidence against Brutus' charge of "ambition"; he informs the crowd of Caesar's intention to give all the poor seventy-five drachmas and free access to his lands; and he calls attention to the pathetic spectacle of Caesar's knife-punctured body, affixing a conspirator's name to each of his wounds. Referring to Brutus repeatedly as "an honorable man," he manages subtly to imply the opposite. In careful stages, Mark Antony succeeds in winning back the crowd's sympathy for Caesar, and in turning them against Brutus, all the while denying that he has any intention of doing so. By the end of the scene, the crowd is clamoring for Brutus' blood and setting out to burn his house down. "Revenge!" they shout. "About! Seek! Burn! Fire! Kill! Slay! Let not a traitor live!" In the short scene that follows (**Act III, scene 3**) we see the frenzied crowd violently attacking the poet Cinna, mistaking him for one of the conspirators against Caesar.

These scenes, Act III, scenes 2 and 3, form the decisive turning point in the play and they have been variously commented upon. From the variety of arguments, two generalizations can safely be made. First, the scene must be read as a striking illustration of a theme that preoccupies Shakespeare throughout his work—the power of rhetoric. Mark Antony emerges in this scene as an equal of such characters as Iago or Hamlet or Richard III in his ability to manipulate people's ideas and feelings by sheer mastery of language. It is not surprising that a writer with Shakespeare's remarkable skill with words should have been interested in the powerful uses to which such a skill could be put. Connected to this theme is the issue of the malleability of the crowd. Shakespeare seems to be demonstrating a rather low opinion of democracy by representing the people at large in this scene as easy victims of Brutus' and Anthony's rhetorical art. Their rapid shift from one extreme view to the other suggests that the unrefined mass of people are incapable of thinking rationally or consistently about political issues but are rather subject to the passions and whims of the moment. This was a view frequently voiced by opponents of democracy in Shakespeare's day. Shakespeare here seems to be supporting this aristocratic view, especially by adding the apparently extraneous short scene in which the crowd mistakenly attacks the poet Cinna. On the whole, the political entity Shakespeare refers to variously as "the crowd," "the people," or "the plebians" comes across as emotionally volatile, easily manipulated, and potentially savage. To the extent that the people are crucial players in the game, Shakespeare seems to suggest, politics will always be more a matter of passion than of reason.

Mark Antony takes the first step toward success in this scene because he shows a superior ability to appeal to people's passions. The tragic failure of Brutus is that he relies too much on an elevated sense of reason and restraint in his political dealings.

The plot begins to move very quickly after this decisive scene. In the beginning of the next act (**Act IV, scene 1**) Antony, Octavius, and Lepidus meet in Antony's house to plot their revenge on the conspirators. (We know from history that after the death of Julius Caesar these three men briefly divided the Roman empire among themselves. Lepidus was quickly pushed aside, and Octavius, Julius Caesar's nephew, eventually defeated Mark Antony at Actium and became Rome's greatest emperor.) Their list of who must die includes not only the entire group of conspirators, but even some of their own relatives. Antony's contempt for Lepidus soon becomes apparent, but Octavius defends Lepidus' loyalty. In contrast to the ethical reflectiveness and high-mindedness of Brutus and his friends, the mood among this group is one of raw and ruthless power-seeking.

The focus shifts to Brutus in the next scene (**Act IV, scene 2**) as he and his army await Cassius and his men near Sardis. Brutus' philosophical calm unravels slightly as he begins to doubt Cassius' commitment to their cause. Cassius soon arrives with his army, however, and takes strong offense at Brutus' doubts. They retire to their tents to discuss their disagreement.

The next scene (**Act IV, scene 3**) takes place entirely within Brutus' tent near Sardis. It begins with Cassius and Brutus arguing heatedly. Brutus accuses Cassius of having "an itchy palm"—of selling off positions within his army for money—and refuses to have any part of this. Cassius is deeply insulted. Claiming that Brutus is falsely accusing him and paying undue attention to his faults, he threatens to kill himself rather than to allow himself to be dishonored in the eyes of his most beloved friend. Brutus relents, and they both ask one another's forgiveness for their rash tempers. Brutus confesses that the reason for his uncharacteristic ill temper is that Portia has died. She killed herself, he explains, in despair, believing that Brutus would not return and that the army of Octavius and Antony was too strong to be defeated. Titinius and Messala enter at this point to inform Brutus and Cassius that Mark Antony, Lepidus, and Octavius are approaching by way of Philippi and that they have put to death one hundred senators, including the great orator Cicero. Brutus proposes that they should march directly on Philippi, in the hope of taking the armies of Antony by surprise before they have time to enlist more men. The tide, Brutus argues, is now with us, but it will soon shift. Cassius initially argues against this plan but then defers to Brutus. They say good night amicably, wishing for no further discord between them. As Brutus sits up reading in his tent that night, the ghost of Caesar appears to him, saying he will see him the next day at Phillipi. Brutus addresses the ghost calmly, then wakes his attendants to ask if they have seen anything. They say no, and he returns to his cot to try to get some sleep.

Act V consists principally of the reactions of Brutus and Cassius to the battle with Octavius, Lepidus, and Mark Antony at Philippi. Put simply, the battle goes very badly for the conspirators, and they both kill themselves rather than allow themselves to be taken prisoner by the enemy. As befits his greatness of character, Brutus' suicide is more dramatic. He tries to persuade two of his men to hold the sword for him, but they refuse out of love for him. He finally convinces Strabo to help him, and his dying words are consistent with the stoic dignity he maintained throughout the play: "Farewell, good Strabo," he says as he falls on his sword. "Caesar, now be still, / I killed not thee with half so good a will." Antony and Octavius arrive on the scene immediately following Brutus' death, and Antony, ironically, gives the great eulogy that closes the play:

> This was the noblest Roman of them all.
> All the conspirators, save only he,
> Did what they did in envy of great Caesar;
> He, only in general honest thought
> And common good to all, made one of them.
> His life was gentle, and the elements
> So mixed in him that Nature might stand up,
> And say to all the world, "This was a man."

The speech recapitulates some of the major themes of the play: Brutus' ethical purity and the frustration of his high standards by the savagery of politics; the tendency of envy and resentment to tarnish and demean human excellence; and the flawed and "mixed" nature of human personality, such that even the noblest aims of reason can be undermined by the unpredictable play of passion. ❖

—*Neal Dolan*
Harvard University

List of Characters

Brutus is the central character of the play, a universally admired and respected nobleman directly descended from Cato—one of Republican Rome's greatest heroes. Hoping that his moral authority will add luster to the cause, Cassius attempts to enlist Brutus in a conspiracy to kill Julius Caesar after Caesar defeats Pompey and returns to Rome in the first stage of the Roman civil wars. Brutus' ethical deliberations about whether or not to join in the conspiracy provide the focus of the first half of the play. He eventually takes a leading role in killing Caesar, but his armies are then defeated in the ensuing battle with Octavius and Mark Antony. He kills himself rather than allow himself to be captured. He is famously eulogized by Mark Antony at the end of the play as "the noblest Roman of them all."

Cassius is Brutus' closest friend and the principal catalyst of the plot to assassinate Caesar. Motivated both by envy of Caesar and by love for the Republic, he is an intense and driven figure. Like Brutus, he falls on his sword rather than allow himself to be taken prisoner after his armies are routed by those of Octavius, Mark Antony, and Lepidus.

Mark Antony is Julius Caesar's right-hand man. A brilliant rhetorician, he successfully turns the crowd against the conspirators at Julius Caesar's funeral. He then joins with Octavius and Lepidus to murder one hundred senators and to defeat the armies of Brutus and Cassius at Philippi.

Julius Caesar is a great general who returns to Rome with ambitions for monarchical power after defeating Pompey in the first stage of the Roman civil wars. His ascent to dictatorial stature is resented and resisted by Brutus and Cassius, among others, who successfully conspire to assassinate him. Shakespeare presents him as a shrewd, balanced, but somewhat vain and arrogant figure.

Octavius is the nephew of Julius Caesar. A successful general, he joins forces with Mark Antony to take power after the death of Julius Caesar. (In Roman history, he renames himself Augustus and becomes the first great emperor of Rome. His reign represents the end of the era of Republican Rome.)

Portia is the wife of Brutus. She is presented as virtuous and loving, with a strong and independent will of her own. She insists that Brutus confide in her as an equal. She despairs of Brutus' chances against the armies of Octavius and Mark Antony and kills herself.

Calphurnia is the wife of Julius Caesar. Unlike her husband, she gives credence to the predictions of prophets and soothsayers and unsuccessfully attempts to dissuade Caesar from going to the Senate on the day he is assassinated.

Decius Brutus is one of the conspirators against Julius Caesar. He goes to Caesar and successfully persuades him to go to the Senate on the day of his assassination. Caesar had heeded the fears of his wife and decided not to go, but Decius convinces him that he will be laughed at and that the senators might reconsider their decision to offer him a crown.

Lepidus is the weakest member of the triumvirate, including Mark Antony and Octavius, that takes power after the death of Julius Caesar. Mark Antony scorns him, but Octavius defends his loyalty.

Cinna is a harmless poet. Mistakenly taken for a conspirator by the same name, he is set upon by the crowd roused to fury at Caesar's funeral by Mark Antony. ✤

Critical Views

[John Dryden (1631–1700), aside from being the greatest English poet of the later seventeenth century, was a pioneer in literary criticism. Among his important critical works are *Of Dramatick Poesie* (1668) and *Of Heroick Plays* (1672). In the following poem, written as a prologue to a production of *Julius Caesar,* Dryden stresses Shakespeare's "artless beauty" and contrasts him with the learned productions of Ben Jonson (1572–1637), who admired Shakespeare but criticized the fact that he knew "little Latin and less Greek."]

In Country Beauties as we often see,
Something that takes in their simplicity;
Yet while they charm, they know not they are fair,
And take without the spreading of the snare;
Such Artless beauty lies in *Shakespears* wit,
'Twas well in spight of him what ere he writ.
His Excellencies came and were not sought,
His words like casual Atoms made a thought:
Drew up themselves in Rank and File, and writ,
He wondring how the Devil it was such wit.
Thus like the drunken Tinker, in his Play,
He grew a Prince, and never knew which way.
He did not know what trope or Figure meant,
But to perswade is to be eloquent,
So in this *Caesar* which to day you see,
Tully ne'r spoke as he makes *Anthony.*
Those then that tax his Learning are to blame,
He knew the thing, but did not know the Name:
Great *Iohnson* did that Ignorance adore,
And though he envi'd much, admir'd him more;
The faultless *Iohnson* equally writ well,
Shakespear made faults; but then did more excel.
One close at Guard like some old Fencer lay,
T'other more open, but he shew'd more play.
In Imitation *Iohnsons* wit was shown,
Heaven made his men; but *Shakespear* made his own.
Wise Iohnson's talent in observing lay,
But others follies still made up his play.
He drew the life in each elaborate line,
But *Shakespear* like a Master did design.

Iohnson with skill dissected humane kind,
And show'd their faults that they their faults might find:
But then as all Anatomists must do,
He to the meanest of mankind did go,
And took from Gibbets such as he would show.
Both are so great that he must boldly dare,
Who both of 'em does judge and both compare.
If amongst Poets one more bold there be,
The man that dare attempt in either way, is he.

—John Dryden, "Prologue to *Julius Caesar*" (1672), *The Poems of John Dryden,* ed. James Kinsley (Oxford: Clarendon Press, 1958), Vol. 1, pp. 142–43

❖

AUGUST WILHELM VON SCHLEGEL ON THE CHARACTER OF CAESAR

[August Wilhelm von Schlegel (1767–1845) was a leading German critic who significantly influenced many English writers of the Romantic period. In his famous book, *Lectures on Dramatic Art and Literature* (1809), excerpted here, Schlegel notes the fact that Caesar has only a relatively small part in *Julius Caesar* but nevertheless seems to dominate the play.]

⟨. . .⟩ the piece of *Julius Caesar,* to complete the action, requires to be continued to the fall of Brutus and Cassius. Caesar is not the hero of the piece, but Brutus. The amiable beauty of this character, his feeling and patriotic heroism, are portrayed with peculiar care. Yet the poet has pointed out with great nicety the superiority of Cassius over Brutus in independent volition and discernment in judging of human affairs; that the latter from the purity of his mind and his conscientious love of justice, is unfit to be the head of a party in a state entirely corrupted; and that these very faults give an unfortunate turn to the cause of the conspirators. In the part of Caesar several ostentatious speeches have been censured as unsuitable. But as he never appears in action, we have no other measure of his greatness than the impression which he makes upon the rest of the characters, and his peculiar confidence in himself. In this Caesar was by no means deficient, as we learn from history and his own writings; but he displayed it more in the easy ridicule of his enemies than in pompous discourses. The theatrical effect of this play is injured by a partial falling off of the last two acts compared with the preceding in external splendour and rapidity. The first appearance of Caesar in festal robes, when the music stops, and all are silent whenever he opens his mouth, and when the few words which he utters are received as oracles, is truly magnificient; the conspiracy is a true conspiracy, which in stolen interviews and in the dead of night prepares the blow which is to be struck in open day, and which is to change the constitution of the world;—the confused thronging before the murder of Caesar, the general agitation even of the perpetrators after the deed, are all portrayed with most masterly skill; with the funeral procession and the speech of Antony the effect reaches its utmost height. Caesar's shade is more powerful to avenge his fall than he himself was to guard against it. After the overthrow of the external splendour and greatness of the conqueror and ruler of the world, the intrinsic grandeur of character of Brutus and Cassius is all that remain to fill the stage and occupy the minds of the spectators: suitably to their name, as the last of the Romans, they stand there, in some degree alone; and the forming a great and hazardous determination is more powerfully calculated to excite our expectation, than the supporting the consequences of the deed with heroic firmness.

> —August Wilhelm von Schlegel, *Letters on Dramatic Art and Literature* (1809), tr. John Black (1816; rpt. London: Henry G. Bohn, 1846), pp. 415–16

❖

H. N. Hudson on Shakespeare's Understanding of Caesar

[H. N. Hudson (1814–1886) was a prolific American critic and compiler of many editions of Shakespeare's plays. Among his many works are *Lectures on Shakespeare* (1848) and *Text-Book of Poetry* (1875). In this extract, taken from his late study, *Shakespeare: His Life, Art and Characters* (1872), Hudson finds that Shakespeare had been fascinated with Caesar for years and had referred to him in several other plays; but Hudson concludes that Shakespeare somehow did not fully portray Caesar's greatness in *Julius Caesar*.]

The characterization of this drama ⟨*Julius Caesar*⟩ in some of the parts is, I confess, not a little perplexing to me. I do not feel quite sure as to the temper of mind in which the Poet conceived some of the persons, or why he should have given them the aspect they wear in the play. For instance, Caesar is far from being himself in these scenes; hardly one of the speeches put into his mouth can be regarded as historically characteristic; taken all together, they are little short of a downright caricature. As here represented, he is indeed little better than a grand, strutting piece of puff-paste; and when he speaks, it is very much in the style of a glorious vapourer and braggart, full of lofty airs and mock-thunder; than which nothing could be further from the truth of the man, whose character, even in his faults, was as compact and solid as adamant, and at the same time as limber and ductile as the finest gold. Certain critics have seized and worked upon this, as proving that Shakespeare must have been very green in classical study, or else very careless in the use of his authorities. To my thinking it proves neither the one nor the other.

It is true, Caesar's ambition was indeed gigantic, but none too much so, I suspect, for the mind it dwelt in; for his character in all its features was gigantic. And no man ever framed his ambition more in sympathy with the great forces of Nature, or built it upon a deeper foundation of political wisdom and insight. Now this "last infirmity of noble minds" is the only part of him that the play really sets before us; and even this we do not see as it was, because it is here severed from the constitutional peerage of his gifts and virtues; all those transcendant qualities which placed him at the summit of Roman intellect and manhood being either withheld from the scene, or thrown so far into the background, that the proper effect of them is mainly lost.

Yet we have ample proof that Shakespeare understood Caesar thoroughly; and that he regarded him as "the noblest man that ever lived in the tide of times." For example, in *Hamlet,* he makes Horatio, who is one of his calmest and most right-thinking characters, speak of him as "the mightiest Julius." In *Antony and Cleopatra,* again, the heroine is made to describe him as "broad-fronted Caesar." And in *King Richard the Third,* the young Prince utters these lines:

> That Julius Caesar was a famous man;
> With what his valour did enrich his wit,
> His wit set down to make his valour live:
> Death makes no conquest of this conqueror.

In fact, we need not go beyond Shakespeare to gather that Julius Caesar's was the deepest, the most versatile, and most multitudinous head that ever figured in the political affairs of mankind.

Indeed, it is clear from this play itself that the Poet's course did not proceed at all from ignorance or misconception of the man. For it is remarkable that, though Caesar delivers himself so out of character, yet others, both foes and friends, deliver him much nearer the truth; so that, while we see almost nothing of him directly, we nevertheless get, upon the whole, a pretty just reflection of him. Especially, in the marvellous speeches of Antony and in the later events of the drama, both his inward greatness and his right of mastership over the Roman world are fully vindicated. For, in the play as in the history, Caesar's blood just hastens and cements the empire which the conspirators thought to prevent. They soon find that in the popular sympathies, and even in their own dumb remorses, he has "left behind powers that will work for him." He proves indeed far mightier in death than in life; as if his spirit were become at once the guardian angel of his cause and an avenging angel to his foes.

And so it was in fact. For nothing did so much to set the people in love with royalty, both name and thing, as the reflection that their beloved Caesar, the greatest of their national heroes, the crown and consummation of Roman genius and character, had been murdered for aspiring to it. This their hereditary aversion to kingship was all subdued by the remembrance of how and why their Caesar fell; and they who, before, would have plucked out his heart rather than he should wear a crown, would now have plucked out their own, to set a crown upon his head. Such is the natural result when the intensities of admiration and compassion meet together in the human breast.

From all which it may well be thought that Caesar was too great for the hero of a drama, since his greatness, if brought forward in full measure, would leave no room for any thing else, at least would preclude any proper dramatic balance and equipoise. It was only as a sort of underlying potency of a force withdrawn into the background, that his presence was compatible with that harmony and reciprocity of several characters which a well-ordered drama requires. At all events, it is pretty clear that, where he was, such figures as Brutus and Cassius could never be very considerable, save as his assassins. They would not have been heard of in aftertimes, if they had not "struck the foremost man of all this world"; in other words, the great sun of Rome had to be shorn of his beams, else so ineffectual a fire as Brutus could nowise catch the eye.

Be this as it may, I have no doubt that Shakespeare knew the whole height and compass of Caesar's vast and varied capacity. And I sometimes regret that he did not render him as he evidently saw him, inasmuch as he alone perhaps of all the men who ever wrote could have given an adequate expression of that colossal man.

—H. N. Hudson, *Shakespeare: His Life, Art and Characters*
(Boston: Ginn & Co., 1872), Vol. 2, pp. 234–37

❖

EDWARD DOWDEN ON MARK ANTONY

[Edward Dowden (1843–1913) was a renowned and voluminous British critic who wrote *A History of French Literature* (1910), *Essays Modern and Elizabethan*

(1910), and biographies of Percy Bysshe Shelley (1886) and Robert Browning (1904). In this extract from his famous 1875 study of Shakespeare, Dowden focuses on the figure of Mark Antony, whose frivolity and lack of purpose will lead to his downfall.]

Antony is a man of genius without moral fibre; a nature of a rich, sensitive, pleasure-loving kind; the prey of good impulses and of bad; looking on life as a game, in which he has a distinguished part to play, and playing that part with magnificent grace and skill. He is capable of personal devotion (though not of devotion to an idea), and has indeed a gift for subordination,—subordination to a Julius Caesar, to a Cleopatra. And as he has enthusiasm about great personalities, so he has a contempt for inefficiency and ineptitude. Lepidus is to him "a slight, unmeritable man meet to be sent on errands," one that is to be talked of not as a person, but as a property. Antony possesses no constancy of self-esteem; he can drop quickly out of favour with himself; and being without reverence for his own type of character, and being endowed with a fine versatility of perception and feeling, he can admire qualities the most remote from his own. It is Antony who utters the *éloge* over the body of Brutus at Philippi. Antony is not without an aesthetic sense and imagination, though of a somewhat unspiritual kind: he does not judge men by a severe moral code, but he feels in an aesthetic way the grace, the splendour, the piteous interest of the actors in the exciting drama of life, or their impertinence, ineptitude and comicality; and he feels that the play is poorer by the loss of so noble a figure as that of a Brutus. But Brutus, over whom his ideals dominate, and who is blind to facts which are not in harmony with his theory of the universe, is quite unable to perceive the power for good or for evil that is lodged in Antony, and there is in the great figure of Antony nothing which can engage or interest his imagination; for Brutus's view of life is not imaginative, or pictorial, or dramatic; but wholly ethical. The fact that Antony abandons himself to pleasure, is "gamesome," reduces him in the eyes of Brutus to a very ordinary person,—one who is silly or stupid enough not to recognise the first principle of human conduct, the need of self-mastery; one against whom the laws of the world must fight, and who is therefore of no importance. And

Brutus was right with respect to the ultimate issues for Antony. Sooner or later Antony must fall to ruin. But before the moral defect in Antony's nature destroyed his fortune much was to happen. Before Actium might come Philippi.

—Edward Dowden, *Shakspere: A Critical Study of His Life and Art* (London: H. S. King, 1875), pp. 289–90

❖

M. W. MacCallum on Shakespeare's Adaptation of Plutarch

[M. W. MacCallum (1854–1942) was an Australian scholar who, aside from such works as *Studies in Low German and High German Literature* (1884) and *Tennyson's* Idylls of the King *and Arthurian Story from the XVIth Century* (1894), wrote a celebrated study of Shakespeare's Roman plays, excerpted here. MacCallum, studying Shakespeare's adaptation of Plutarch's life of Caesar, believes that Shakespeare infused his characters with powerful sentiments that were not Roman but that produced vital dramatic conflict.]

Shakespeare's position may be thus described. He read in Plutarch that Brutus, the virtuous Roman, killed Caesar, the master-spirit of his own and perhaps of any age, from a disinterested sense of duty. That was easy to understand, for Shakespeare would know, and if he did not know it from his own experience his well-conned translation of Montaigne would teach him, that the best of men are determined in their feeling of right by the preconceptions of race, class, education and the like. But he also read that Brutus was a philosophic student who would not accept or obey the current code without scrutinising it and fitting it into his theory. Of the political theory, however, which such an one would have, Shakespeare had no knowledge or appreciation. So whenever Brutus tries to harmonise his purpose with his idealist doctrine, he has to be furnished with new reasons instead of the old and obvious ones. And these are neither very clear nor very antique. They make one inclined to quote concerning him the words of Caesar spoken to Cicero in regard to the historical Brutus:

> I knowe not what this young man woulde, but what he woulde he willeth it vehemently.   (*Marcus Brutus.*)

For what is it that he would? The one argument with which he can excuse to his own heart the projected murder, is that the aspirant to royal power, though hitherto irreproachable, may or must become corrupted and misuse his high position. This is as different from the attitude of the ancient Roman as it well could be. It would never have occurred to the genuine republican of olden time that any justification was needed for despatching a man who sought to usurp the sovereign place; and if it had, this is certainly the last justification that would have entered his head.

But the introspection, the self-examination, the craving for an inward moral sanction that will satisfy the conscience, and the choice of the particular sanction that does so, are as typical of the modern as they are alien to the classical mind. It is clear that an addition of this kind is not merely mechanical or superficial. It affects the elements already given, and produces, as it were, a new chemical combination. And this particular instance shows how Shakespeare transforms the whole story. He reanimates Brutus by infusing into his veins a strain of present feeling that in some ways transmutes his character; and, transmuting the character in which the chief interest centres, he cannot leave the other *data* as they were. He can resuscitate the past in its persons, its conflicts, its palpitating vitality just because he endows it with his own life. It was an ancient belief that the shades of the departed were inarticulate or dumb till they had lapped a libation of warm blood; then they would speak forth their secrets. In like manner it is the life-blood of Shakespeare's own passion and thought that throbs in the pulses of these unsubstantial dead and gives them human utterance once more. This, however, has two aspects. It is the dead who speak; but they speak through the life that Shakespeare has lent them. The past is resuscitated; but it is a resuscitation, not the literal existence it had before. Nor in any

other way can the phantoms of history win bodily shape and
perceptible motion for the world of breathing men.

—M. W. MacCallum, "The Titular Hero of the Play,"
Shakespeare's Roman Plays and Their Background (London:
Macmillan, 1910), pp. 205–7

❖

GEORGE BERNARD SHAW ON SHAKESPEARE'S PORTRAYAL OF
CAESAR

[George Bernard Shaw (1856–1950), the greatest
British playwright of his age, was naturally influenced
by Shakespeare in his own play, *Caesar and Cleopatra*
(included in *Three Plays for Puritans,* 1901). But Shaw
always maintained a somewhat ambivalent and even
hostile attitude to Shakespeare, perhaps as a way of
differentiating himself from his great predecessor. In
this extract, Shaw questions whether Shakespeare was
capable of portraying a genuinely great individual such
as Julius Caesar.]

In Caesar, I have used another character with which Shakespear
has been beforehand. But Shakespear, who knew human weakness so well, never knew human strength of the Caesarian
type. His Caesar is an admitted failure: his Lear is a master-
piece. The tragedy of disillusion and doubt, of the agonized
struggle for a foothold on the quicksand made by an acute
observation striving to verify its vain attribution of morality and
respectability to Nature, of the faithless will and the keen eyes
that the faithless will is too weak to blind: all this will give you
a Hamlet or a Macbeth, and win you great applause from literary gentlemen; but it will not give you a Julius Caesar. Caesar
was not in Shakespear, nor in the epoch, now fast waning,
which he inaugurated. It cost Shakespear no pang to write
Caesar down for the merely technical purpose of writing Brutus
up. And what a Brutus! A perfect Girondin, mirrored in
Shakespear's art two hundred years before the real thing came
to maturity and talked and stalked and had its head duly cut off

by the coarser Antonys and Octaviuses of its time, who at least knew the difference between life and rhetoric.

It will be said that these remarks can bear no other construction than an offer of my Caesar to the public as an improvement of Shakespear's. And in fact, that is their precise purport. But here let me give a friendly warning to those scribes who have so often exclaimed against my criticisms of Shakespear as blasphemies against a hitherto unquestioned Perfection and Infallibility. Such criticisms are no more new than the creed of my Diabolonian Puritan or my revival of the humors of Cool as a Cucumber. Too much surprise at them betrays an acquaintance with Shakespear criticism so limited as not to include even the prefaces of Dr Johnson and the utterances of Napoleon. I have merely repeated in the dialect of my own time and in the light of its philosophy what they said in the dialect and light of theirs. Do not be misled by the Shakespear fanciers who, ever since his own time, have delighted in his plays just as they might have delighted in a particular breed of pigeons if they had never learnt to read. His genuine critics, from Ben Jonson to Mr Frank Harris, have always kept as far on this side idolatry as I.

> —George Bernard Shaw, "Better Than Shakespear?" (preface to *Three Plays for Puritans*) (1901), *The Works of Bernard Shaw* (London: Constable, 1930), Vol. 9, pp. xxxii–xxxiii

❖

G. WILSON KNIGHT ON THE IDEA OF CAESAR

[G. Wilson Knight (1897–1939), a leading British Shakespeare scholar, taught drama and English literature at the University of Leeds. He was the author of many volumes of criticism, including *The Wheel of Fire* (1930), *The Starlit Dome* (1941), *The Crown of Life* (1947), and *Shakespeare and Religion* (1967). In this extract, taken from an essay in *The Imperial Theme* (1931), Knight believes that in *Julius Caesar* the idea of Caesar—the notion that Caesar is a kind of superhuman figure—is greater than Caesar himself.]

The figure of Julius Caesar ⟨in Shakespeare's *Julius Caesar*⟩ stands out, brilliant. From the start he is idealized in point of power, general respect, glory. His failing must not receive our only attention: he is endued dramatically with strength, importance, almost divinity. He is a sublime figure-head, but, the general acclamations at any time stilled, we see him as a man, weak, egotistical, petulant. But his weakness must not prevent our recognition of power behind such words as Cassius'

> Why, man, he doth bestride the narrow world
> Like a Colossus . . .   (I. ii. 135)

The Caesar-idea is accompanied by all the usual Shakespearian suggestions of world-glory and life-beauty. Here they are raised to a high pitch. The men of Rome put on their best 'attire' (I. i. 53) for his triumph, 'strew flowers in his way' (I. i. 55). His images are robed and decked with his 'trophies' and 'ceremonies' (I. i. 69–74). Every one's attention hangs on his words:

> Peace, ho! Caesar speaks.   (I. ii. 1)

His entry is accompanied with music. He is associated with images of infinity, the North Star and Olympus (III. i. 60, 74). He is, as it were, a frail man buoyed on the full flood of success. He is conscious of his own triumphant destiny:

> . . . danger knows full well
> That Caesar is more dangerous than he:
> We are two lions litter'd in one day,
> And I the elder and more terrible.   (II. ii. 44)

The idea of Caesar is ever far greater here than Caesar the man. It is so to Caesar himself. He has an almost superstitious respect for his own star, and is afraid of acting unworthy of it: thus he here persuades himself not to show fear, since he is greater than danger itself. Often he has to persuade himself in this fashion:

> Shall Caesar send a lie?
> Have I in conquest stretch'd mine arm so far,
> To be afeard to tell greybeards the truth?   (II. ii. 65)

This shortly follows his words, 'Mark Antony shall say I am not well' (II. ii. 55): either because now Decius is present, or purely due to his sudden attempt to live up to the Caesar-idea. He often vacillates like this. He tells Antony that Cassius is a danger, then pulls himself up sharply with 'Always, I am Caesar' (I. ii. 212). We are, indeed, aware of two Caesars: the ailing and petulant old man, and the giant spirit standing colossal over the Roman Empire to be. There is an insubstantial, mirage-like uncertainty about this Caesar. How are we to see him? He is two incompatibles, shifting, interchanging. As the hour of his death draws near, this induces almost a sickening feeling, like a ship's rocking. This is the uncertainty, the unreal phantasma, of Brutus' mind, and, for a while, of ours. Caesar is himself, curiously, aware of both his selves: hence his rapid changes, his admixture of fine phrases resonant of imperial glory with trivialities, platitudes, absurdities. Confronted by Metellus Cimber's petition, he is intent, not on justice, but on preserving his own constancy. The North Star alone remains constant in the skies, and Caesar must be such a star to men:

> So in the world; 'tis furnish'd well with men,
> And men are flesh and blood, and apprehensive;
> Yet in the number I do know but one
> That unassailable holds on his rank,
> Unshaked of motion; and that I am he,
> Let me a little show it, even in this,
> That I was constant Cimber should be banish'd,
> And constant do remain to keep him so.   (III. i. 66)

He wants primarily to 'show' his constancy: to the world, to himself. He must prove its existence. His egotism thus knows no bounds. And yet his egotism is both compelling and ludicrous. The baffling coexistence of these elements in single speeches, single phrases even, is remarkable: there is nothing quite like it in Shakespeare. He can say with finality, 'Caesar doth not wrong' (III. i. 47). Petitions may 'fire the blood of ordinary men' but not Caesar's (III. i. 37). All this may seem a little foolish: yet if we see only foolishness, we are wrong. We must observe both Caesars, keep both ever in mind: one physical and weak, the other all but supernatural in spiritual power, a power blazing in the fine hyperboles of his egocentricity. Cassius notes how superstitions now affect Caesar:

> For he is superstitious grown of late,
> Quite from the main opinion he held once
> Of fantasy, of dreams, and ceremonies.   (II. i. 195)

This is not surprising: it is a normal correlative to his superstitious respect for his idealized self. Nor, in this world, is superstition a fault: it is fully justified. Moreover Cassius himself (V. i. 77–9) and Calpurnia (II. ii. 13–14) express elsewhere an exactly similar change towards superstition. The Soothsayer's prophecy comes true. Dreams and auguries are justified by the event; portents are ever faithful harbingers of destruction. Caesar's ghost appears twice to Brutus, and he knows his hour has come (V. v. 17–20). We are vividly conscious of the supernatural. Thus Caesar's superstition and almost superstitious respect for his own importance are, in this universe, not irrational. Again, we are pointed to the root ideas here: physical weakness, spiritual energy, the supernatural. And this spiritual element burns fierce in the almost divine glory to which Caesar tries pathetically to adjust himself. Whatever it be, this Caesar-idea, it is more powerful than Caesar the man. It controls him while he lives, survives and avenges him after his death. 'The spirit of Caesar' is not reached by slaying Caesar's body: it rather gains strength thereafter. Therefore, whatever we may think of Caesar as a man, we must see him also as a symbol of something of vast import, resplendent majesty, and starry purpose.

—G. Wilson Knight, "The Eroticism of *Julius Caesar*," *The Imperial Theme* (1931; 3rd ed. London: Methuen, 1951), pp. 64–66

❖

HAROLD S. WILSON ON SHAKESPEARE'S INTERPRETATION OF HISTORY

[Harold S. Wilson (b. 1904) is the author of *On the Design of Shakespearian Tragedy* (1957), from which the following extract is taken. Here, Wilson shows that

Julius Caesar is a logical development from Shakespeare's earlier English history plays in its study of human nature in an historical context.]

The play centres upon what Shakespeare's age probably considered the most famous event of ancient history, as it was set forth in the pages of their favourite moralist among the ancient historians, whom Shakespeare read in Sir Thomas North's fine version. It was a theme full of political and moral import for Shakespeare's time, the story of the assassination of a dictator, the grandeur of whose personality has impressed succeeding ages like that of no other man. Caesar's murder changed the mightiest of states from a republic of free men who ruled the world to an empire which rapidly degenerated into tyranny. So Shakespeare endeavoured to comprehend it.

His task, in constructing a tragedy upon this theme, was one of historical interpretation. Undoubtedly Shakespeare made a careful effort of historical imagination for *Julius Caesar* and his other Roman plays, thinking himself back into the time of Cicero and Brutus, Cleopatra and Octavius Caesar, Aufidius and Coriolanus, trying to feel their motives and to think their thoughts, as he found them suggested in Plutarch. Shakespeare's Romans are by no means Elizabethans; they are *men,* of course, as Dr. Johnson remarked; for Shakespeare, human nature is universally the same; but Shakespeare's Romans do not have the outlook and attitudes of Christians, nor do they recognize the same political motives and values as Elizabethans, or share recognizably kindred tastes. Shakespeare, in fact, is very careful in *Julius Caesar* and the other Roman plays to avoid anachronisms—witness the difference in such plays as *Troilus and Cressida* (where the atmosphere is mediaeval) or in *The Winter's Tale* (where anachronism seems to be a calculated part of the effect). He is not so learned as Ben Jonson; there is no special attempt to create historical atmosphere; but Shakespeare is clearly trying to interpret the actual motives and point of view of historical persons in *Julius Caesar, Antony and Cleopatra,* and *Coriolanus,* to make us understand, with his artist's imagination, how the events which Plutarch records, in his interesting but limited historian's way, really came about. He takes minor liberties with

Plutarch's data—especially with the chronology, in the service of his dramatic narrative—as he did with the events of the English history plays; but he is remarkably faithful, on the whole, to the main lines of Plutarch's narrative, even to the extent of transferring whole passages of North's prose into verse, almost word for word, as has often been remarked.

To the writing of *Julius Caesar,* Shakespeare brought the rich experience of the English history plays he had already produced. *Julius Caesar* belongs to the period of the two parts of *Henry IV* and *Henry V* and contains minor reminiscences of *1 Henry IV.* There is the same effort of historical imagination; but *Julius Caesar* lacks the immediacy and warmth of patriotic feeling that we sense throughout the plays dealing with English history. There is a cool detachment about *Julius Caesar,* a dispassionate study of incident and motive and character. Human nature is displayed with profound insight, as always with Shakespeare; but the actors move in a context of political concepts in some degree alien to Shakespeare the Elizabethan and patriot of the English histories; and there is a pervasive irony, characteristic of Shakespeare's dealings with antiquity generally, which controls the mood of the whole.

In this mood of ironic contemplation, of disinterested reflection upon the great persons and happenings of an age that had vanished, Shakespeare follows the pattern of events with a clear and untroubled gaze. It is a pattern of moral causes and their effects in this world. There are no theological, no metaphysical preconceptions. The world of *Julius Caesar*—as of *Antony and Cleopatra* and *Coriolanus*—is the natural order of man, which is a moral order, but the religious sanction of that order is not invoked. It is simply man's world as he knows it by the light of natural reason—as Plutarch knew it, and Julius Caesar, Brutus, Cassius, and the rest. In this world there are no significant chains of accident, as we have observed them in *Romeo and Juliet* and *Hamlet.* The moments of choice are clear and emphatic: Brutus's soliloquy (II, i), Caesar's disregard of Calphurnia's foreboding dream, Brutus's overbearing Cassius's judgment about Antony and about the battle of Philippi; even the lack of judgment in the Roman mob has its sequent penalty. The action does, of course, imply a superhuman order of

justice and retribution; only we must not think of sin and pun-
ishment, if they carry any Christian implications for us, but
rather of *ate* (the mad folly that comes upon proud men),
hybris (arrogance), and *nemesis* (the inescapable consequences
of *ate* and *hybris*). Shakespeare invokes no other explanation of
events, and even these Greek conceptions we must invoke for
ourselves; but they best fit the course of events in
Shakespeare's Roman plays. What he shows us is a moral pattern of human history, a sequence of human causes and their
effects. The supernatural portents in *Julius Caesar,* even the
ghost of Caesar before Philippi, are not agents in the drama.
They are present for atmospheric effect, and because they figure in Plutarch's account; we may take them as symbolic of the
moral event, or not, as we please; but they do not determine
anything. The moral outcome is clearly enough determined by
the characters of the drama as they feel and think and act
before our eyes.

> —Harold S. Wilson, "Thesis: Julius Caesar and Coriolanus," *On
> the Design of Shakespearian Tragedy* (Toronto: University of
> Toronto Press, 1957), pp. 86–88

❖

H. M. RICHMOND ON SHAKESPEARE'S CAESAR AS AN AGING HERO

[H. M. Richmond (b. 1932) is a professor of English and
director of the Shakespeare program at the University
of California at Berkeley. He has written studies of
Richard III (1989) and *Henry VIII* (1994) as well as
Shakespeare's Sexual Comedy (1971). In this extract,
Richmond maintains that in the character of Caesar,
Shakespeare has found a representation of aging great-
ness.]

It is precisely the purely personal slackening of political acu-
men that Shakespeare has striven to evoke in his aging Julius
Caesar—a portrait of decline drawn at the expense of strict
fidelity to North's translation of Plutarch, on which the drama-

tist depended for most of his details. Caesar is the first of those aging yet still monumental figures, cast in the mold of Sophocles' Oedipus, that preside over many of Shakespeare's mature tragedies: Othello, Lear, Antony. This study shows what happens to a Henry V if he grows old in triumph without perpetually relearning the lesson he so painfully learned before Agincourt. There is still no question, however, of the superiority of Caesar's political instincts to those of all the men around him. His insight into his most dangerous opponent, Cassius, is limited only by the complacent assurance that he no longer needs to act on such judgments:

> . . . if my name were liable to fear,
> I do not know the man I should avoid
> So soon as that spare Cassius. He reads much;
> He is a great observer and he looks
> Quite through the deeds of men; . . .
> Such men as he be never at heart's ease
> Whiles they behold a greater than themselves,
> And therefore are they very dangerous.
> I rather tell thee what is to be fear'd
> Than what I fear; for always I am Caesar.
> Come on my right hand, for this ear is deaf,
> And tell me truly what thou think'st of him.
>
> (I.ii.199–203, 208–14)

There is an economical boldness in the characterization of decaying genius in this speech. Shakespeare stresses the strength of Caesar's insight by setting the passage immediately after Cassius has provocatively vented his resentment at Caesar's power, in his conversation with Brutus:

> Why, man, he doth bestride the narrow world
> Like a Colossus, and we petty men
> Walk under his huge legs and peep about
> To find ourselves dishonourable graves.   (I.ii.135–8)

While Caesar evaluates Cassius with precision, he shows indifference to those immediate advantages that are to be gained by applying such insights to practical purposes (as Cassius does with Brutus) a sign of petrifying political judgment. Caesar's ultimate triumph is shown by Shakespeare to have been accompanied by a decline in flexibility, which is almost always fatal to a politician. Caesar cannot afford not to fear, and the decay of judgment that is implicit in his neglect of such inward perceptions is subtly reinforced by the symptoms of decline in his outward ones, such as his partial deafness (I.ii.213).

There is a subtle augury in the bearing that this loss of effectiveness has on our sense of Caesar's omnipotence, since his dangerous self-assurance echoes that very complacency that is a familiar theme in the censure of Richard II. Caesar feels that his superiority verges on the transcendent; his profound preoccupation with the kingship proffered by Antony suggests how closely he approaches the medieval role of the English kings in Shakespeare's plays. His physical collapse at the climax of this public invitation to accept absolute power reflects the very intensity of this concern and at the same time, once again, the failure of efficiency in a man past his prime, who is no longer able to take decisive action.

—H. M. Richmond, *Shakespeare's Political Plays* (New York: Random House, 1967), pp. 204–6

❖

DAVID LOWENTHAL ON CAESAR AS MARTYR

[David Lowenthal is a professor of political science at Boston College. He has translated Montesquieu's *Greatness of the Romans and Their Decline* (1965) and written articles on Shakespeare, Locke, Orwell, and others. In this extract, Lowenthal believes that Shakespeare's Caesar, who has already achieved domination over Rome, actually engenders his own death so as to become a martyr who will live in history.]

Much dissimulation masks the fact that Caesar's main—perhaps his sole—interest is himself, although his way of talking about himself in the third person and the qualities he lays claim to fairly shout it out. From Cassius we learn that Caesar dared him to swim the raging Tiber with him, and that he bade the Romans to "mark him and write his speeches in their books."

He was, then, highly competitive, sought to do unusually difficult things, and wanted to be remembered long after his death. He clearly prides himself on his vast conquests, and even more, we may presume, on having succeeded in making himself master of Rome as well as of its farflung empire. Shakespeare even goes so far as to demonstrate before our eyes—though most unobtrusively—Caesar's perfectly remarkable capacity for ruling men, and for altering his demeanor from one audience to another. At Lupercal we see him first as lordly emperor, the next moment as self-abasing slave of the people. In one scene afterwards he is the gentlemanly equal of fellow aristocrats, welcoming them into his home that morning, and in the next not only the emperor or king again but the godlike man, like unto the northern star. Where else in literature are the manners befitting such different regimes manifested side by side in so short a space?

Caesar must enjoy this unrivalled and almost uncanny ability to suit style to occasion. But if he is already in fact Rome's king, what remains? If, as Cassius himself admits, he is now become a god, bearing the palm alone, and ". . . doth bestride the narrow world like a Colossus," can we have further ambition? The analysis given by Plutarch, at a place where the events contained in Shakespeare's play begin, is this:

> Caesar was born to do great things, and had a passion after honour, and the many noble exploits he had done did not now serve as an inducement to him to sit still and reap the fruit of his past labours, but were incentives and encouragements to go on, and raised in him ideas of still greater actions, and a desire of new glory, as if the present were all spent. It was in fact a sort of emulous struggle with himself, as it had been with another, how he might outdo his past actions by his future.

Plutarch goes on to say that Caesar planned to add to his glory at this point through a new campaign against the Parthians, an assortment of geographical improvements, and a new calendar, but

> . . . that which brought upon him the most apparent and mortal hatred was his desire of being king; which gave the common people the first occasion to quarrel with him, and proved the most specious pretense to those who had been his secret enemies all along.

In Shakespeare's play only the last of these ambitions shows itself, and most directly in the crown-offering scene recounted by Casca. Why Antony offers a crown or coronet to Caesar at the Feast of Lupercal we are not told. Neither before nor after that scene do he and Caesar discuss the matter, and it is highly improbable that Antony—the Antony of "When Caesar says, 'Do this,' it is performed"—would undertake so important an action without Caesar's explicit direction or consent. We are told by Casca that Caesar put the crown aside reluctantly, and by Brutus (confirmed by Casca) that Caesar came away from the scene looking angry or sad. He seems to have wanted the crown very badly—a conclusion that spurs Brutus to join the conspiracy, and is also drawn by the senate as a whole.

Does Shakespeare's (not Plutarch's) Caesar really wish to become king? That he wants people to think so seems obvious. But what would he gain thereby? With the crown would no doubt come the opportunity to dispense further with republican forms, and perhaps the right to convey his authority either to a natural heir or, lacking that, to one of his own choosing. But a man with Caesar's love of distinction would also see certain disadvantages. Kingship, as traditionally and ordinarily understood in Rome, could never completely free itself from association with the Tarquins and hence from the obloquy in which it was held over many centuries. Moreover, it could hardly bring renown to Caesar as a novel system of his own creation, since its revival would be that of a very old system devised by others. This revived monarchy, finally, would depend on his receiving the consent of the senate and the people, and would, therefore, always retain something of this dependence.

From the viewpoint of a man of the highest ambition—of one of the very few who, according to Abraham Lincoln, belonged to the "family of the lion and the tribe of the eagle"—these were important defects, but how could they be avoided? History provides the answer: Caesar must found a new regime to which he would give his name—the rule of the Caesars—instead. The only change Shakespeare makes is to attribute to Caesar's intention, and to a comprehensive plan, what historically seems to have come about without such a plan, even if by a kind of necessity. Unfortunately—though it will challenge him to a display of fortitude without parallel—Caesar cannot assure the success of this plan without submitting to, and indeed in some degree arranging, his own assassination, martyrdom and deification. Only on this improbable but not impossible assumption can we explain the paradoxes and inconsistencies into which we have otherwise fallen. Only in this way can we explain several subtle changes Shakespeare makes in Plutarch's account of the same events. And only in this way can we make sense of the play being named after Caesar, and of the necessary, rather than accidental, triumph of his spirit, embodied in the forces of Octavius and Antony, that constitutes the primary import and lesson of the second and larger part of the play.

—David Lowenthal, "Shakespeare's Caesar's Plan," *Interpretation* 10, Nos. 2/3 (May & September 1982): 229–31

❖

ANN MOLAN ON THE FIGURE OF BRUTUS

[Ann Molan is a tutor in English at the Australian National University and has written on Shakespeare and Jane Austen. In this extract, Molan studies the character of Brutus, finding him more a shadow than a counterpart of Caesar.]

What we come to learn here is that Brutus obscurely senses himself entirely at the beck of Rome should Rome make a claim on him. More intimately than he can recognize, he senses that there is no separation between himself and Rome. For him, it can never be a matter of a request from Rome followed by an answer from himself. Rather the man whom Rome "entreats" or commissions or addresses is what Brutus most fundamentally knows himself to be. So how could he *not* find it in himself to remove Caesar? We can see why he is so aghast at the process Cassius is setting in motion, and why his habitual bearing in the world denies his susceptibility to anything he can't control. Whatever Rome has in store for him, it will not be some burden placed upon him, or some position he must attempt to fill, or some enterprise to which he must bend his energies. If it were, there would be a refuge, a "real self" to which Brutus could retreat from whatever functions he performs. But such dissociation is not possible for him. This is borne out when he later abjures the oath proposed by Cassius: Brutus can't conceive of any vantage-point outside his answer to Rome from which he could certify that answer. What part of him could he know that is not within it? It would sound in his ears like taking an oath to be Brutus.

What this suggests is that Brutus is a shadow rather than an antithesis of Caesar, and that he becomes an antithesis in fear of his own singularity. There are times when he partly recognizes its power—for example, the way he sends for Caius Ligarius— "He loves me well . . . and I'll fashion him" (II,i,219–20), a prediction borne out by Ligarius's extravagant response: "I follow you, / To do I know not what: but it sufficeth / That Brutus leads me on" (II,i,233–5). Other signs are his instinctive assumption of leadership in the conspiracy, and the clear implication that everything he says is trustworthy because he is Brutus. The quality of Portia's love for him, in going so far beyond the "functions" of a wife, in knowing him as "my Brutus", attests to more in him than his Roman honour. This is clear when she begs to share his secrets, and appeals, in a way that carries complete conviction, to the warm and open intimacy between them. Brutus is loved by a great many in Rome, and the play makes it clear that his primacy in the conspiracy is accorded not because his principles demand respect but because the singular charisma or grace of *his* life draws men's hearts. Brutus is marked out and separate in Rome, and nothing that makes him like other men is more important than that which makes him unique. Casca says that "His countenance, like richest alchemy, / Will change [offence] to virtue and to worthiness" (I,iii,159–60). The oddity of deriving those weighty abstractions from Brutus's face points up the paradox of his life: Brutus is the single man in Rome thought capable of obliterating the singular Caesar. The circling in of the conspirators on Brutus is an analogue of their circling in on Caesar, and has its own terror.

But how does this notion of Brutus square with his being an embodiment of all the Roman virtues? By another paradox: the Rome Shakespeare expects us to know can be understood and judged only on its own terms, being outstanding among the nations and continually outstripping itself. But with Brutus, the shape of his self is reflected or effected in the way he was of putting "Rome" to himself, in the shape he recognizes there. His anticipation of the kind of commission Cassius could bear from Rome clearly indicates the firm contours he needs Rome to have:

> . . . yet I love him well.
> But wherefore do you hold me here so long?
> What is it that you would impart to me?
> If it be aught toward the general good,
> Set honour in one eye, and death i'th'other,
> And I will look on both indifferently;
> For let the gods so speed me as I love
> The name of honour more than I fear death. (I,ii,82–9)

The formality, the lofty rhetorical ring to the expressions and the ponderous rhythm conceive a Rome whose challenges necessarily fall within a certain range: heroic, traditional and impersonal. Nor can Brutus conceive of honour separate from the sacrifice of his life. This is clearly manifested in his will to "look . . . indifferently", as in the unprompted mention of death, and in the superseding of "yet I love [Caesar] well" with "I love / The name of honour". What he is prepared to hear from Rome is an injunction to submerge everything that is strikingly particular, in order to secure what he vaguely signals as "the general good".

Brutus retires to seek some single, encompassing understanding of Rome, himself and Caesar that can accommodate this sense of prodigious magnitude—his own no less than Caesar's. The coherence he needs is that of an unfolding story, where what is now and what is yet to come are implied by what has been, and ordered according to some over-riding general principle. For him, the general good implicit in that principle must be larger than his own capacity to be always "further moved".

—Ann Molan, "Julius Caesar: The General Good and the Singular Case," *Critical Review* 26 (1984): 90–92

❖

[Jacqueline Pearson (b. 1949) is a Lecturer in English
Language and Literature at Victoria University of
Manchester in Manchester, England. She has written
Tragedy and Tragicomedy in the Plays of John Webster
(1980) and *The Prostituted Muse: Images of Women
and Women Dramatists 1642–1737* (1988). In this
extract, Pearson shows that Caesar is seen in many different ways by various characters, with the result that
his greatness is frequently deflated by his ordinary
human qualities.]

From the beginning of ⟨Shakespeare's *Julius Caesar*⟩ Caesar
himself is seen in a multitude of contrasting ways. To Flavius
and Marullus he is a usurper who has come 'in triumph over
Pompey's blood' (I.1.51). Immediately, though, the perspective shifts and we see a Caesar with royal charisma and, at least
according to Antony, not only kingly but godlike, able to create
by his word alone: 'When Caesar says, "Do this," it is perfor-
m'd' (I.2.10). Caesar's complex nature is created by the widely
differing views of him the play presents. To Cassius his personal weakness renders ludicrous his political strength. To Brutus
he is a moderate man never previously swayed by his passions,
but who is a 'serpent's egg' (II.1.32) which may hatch out a
venomous snake. To both he is a usurper. To Antony on the
contrary he is the murdered king, 'royal' (III.1.127), 'most
noble' (III.1.156), 'the noblest man' (III.1.256) whose 'sacred
blood' (III.2.135) has been shed so that destructive civil war
must result. Artemidorus' Caesar is different again, a man
whose crucial quality is his 'virtue' (II.3.11), and who is
destroyed by 'traitors' (II.3.14). None of these views, though, is
to be seen as having absolute validity. Each observer colours
the world by his own political or personal ideals, whether this
is Brutus' conservative democracy or Antony's opportunism.
The audience is invited not to take sides but to assess the situation in all its complexity.

Ironic juxtaposition is also used to create Caesar's moral and
political ambiguity. Caesar the hero is repeatedly deflated by
our glimpses of Caesar the man. At his first appearance his per-

fect control of the situation and Antony's assertion of his god-like power are undermined by our progressive discoveries that he is childless, deaf in one ear, and epileptic. Sometimes the Tamburlainean self-assertions are more ludicrous than impressive: 'Danger knows full well/That Caesar is more dangerous than he' (II.2.44–5). Moreover, Shakespeare so structures the play that Caesar's noblest gestures are immediately undercut. He is offered the crown and rejects it with a splendidly melodramatic gesture: then he has an epileptic fit. He denies that he is one of the mass of 'ordinary men' (III.1.37), but is rather as 'constant as the northern star' (III.1.60). This claim to superhuman stability is shockingly, and at once, disproved by his murder. The man who is more dangerous than danger, who is constant as the northern star, is actually all too ordinary and all too mortal. One of Shakespeare's most powerful ironic devices in the play is this juxtaposition of starkly contrasting details, like the northern star and the bloody corpse.

—Jacqueline Pearson, "Romans and Barbarians: The Structure of Irony in Shakespeare's Roman Tragedies," *Shakespearian Tragedy,* ed. Malcolm Bradbury and David Palmer (London: Edward Arnold, 1984), pp. 162–63

❖

Robert S. Miola on Caesar as a Tyrant

[Robert S. Miola (b. 1951), a professor of English at Loyola College in Baltimore, is the author of *Shakespeare's Rome* (1983), *Shakespeare and Classical Tragedy* (1992), and *Shakespeare and Classical Comedy* (1994). In this extract, Miola claims that although Shakespeare portrays Caesar as a tyrant, he also endows Caesar with many mitigating qualities.]

Although Shakespeare endows Caesar with some of the attributes of a tyrant, he draws the portrait in light and shade, with many qualifying brushstrokes. Caesar may fear plots but he loves and trusts his fellow Romans. He is close to Antony and warmly invites Brutus and the other conspirators to share wine: "Good friends, go in, and taste some wine with me, / And we, like friends, will straightway go together" (II.ii.126–27). How unlike the typical tyrant who lives sequestered from his people, surrounded by a guard of foreign mercenaries. Kindly, he leaves to the people his "private arbors and new-planted orchards, / On this side Tiber" (III.ii.248–49), thus making all citizens "heirs for ever" (250). This provision for the distribution of personal possessions neatly opposes the avarice described in I Sam. 8:14, a passage that portrayed the typical tyrant for many, including Erasmus, Ponet, and Goodman: "And he will take your fieldes, and your vineyardes, and your best olive trees, and give them to his servants." In direct contrast to the typical tyrant's greed, Caesar's posthumous generosity unites all Romans as familial legatees and characterizes him as the magnanimous *pater patriae.* And though, granted, Caesar shows *superbia,* he places self last and others first on at least one crucial occasion. After Artemidorus urges him to read a letter exposing the conspiracy, Caesar responds, "What touches us ourself shall be last serv'd" (III.i.8), and sweeps on to his death. Shakespeare here diverges from Plutarch's account (V, 66), wherein Caesar tries many times to read the letter but cannot because of the crowd; he portrays instead the self-sacrificing ruler more concerned with public welfare than his own.

It is true that Caesar is willful but so are others in the play. Brutus overrules the wishes of his fellows on at least three important decisions: 1) he urges the sparing of Antony; 2) he allows Antony to speak at Caesar's funeral; 3) he meets the enemy at Philippi. In fact, as some have noted, Brutus resembles Caesar in significant ways: both command the respect of Romans, both have night scenes with their wives, both proclaim their honor and Romanitas, both spurn fear of death. In quarrel with Cassius, Brutus sounds the note of self-glorification prominent in Caesar's northern star speech:

> There is no terror, Cassius, in your threats;
> For I am arm'd so strong in honesty
> That they pass by me as the idle wind,
> Which I respect not.   (IV.iii.66–69)

This series of parallels may ironically reveal tyrannical tendencies in the self-proclaimed tyrant-slayer. Yet, it may just as well suggest that Brutus has those qualities of willfullness necessary in any leader, especially in one who undertakes so great a task. Antony, who leads the countermovement of the play, is also willful as is Octavius, who stubbornly defies Antony and holds to the right side of the battlefield, saying "I will do so" (V.i.20).

Upon closer examination then, Shakespeare seems to qualify Caesar's tyrannical characteristics by dramatic context. Caesar refuses clemency but so do many good rulers, we uneasily realize. Brutus says he knows "no personal cause to spurn at him" (II.i.11) and admits his innocence: "to speak truth of Caesar, / I have not known when his affections sway'd / More than his reason" (19–21). He agrees perfectly with Plutarch: "it seemed he [Caesar] rather had the name and opinion onely of a tyranne, then otherwise that he was so in deede. For there never followed any tyrannicall nor cruell act. . . ." (VI, 237). Flatly concluding that the quarrel will "bear no color for the thing he is" (29), Brutus fashions justifications. Later he mentions a record of offences (III.ii.37–40), but we never see it. The conspirators do not make an issue of Caesar's silencing the tribunes and Shakespeare likewise ignores other incriminating material from Plutarch: the bribing of magistrates (V, 31); the dream of incest with his mother (V, 35); the war against Pompey (V, 35ff.); the robbery of Saturn's temple (V, 38); the affair with Cleopatra (V, 50–51); the burning of the library at Alexandria (V, 51); the promotion to "perpetuall Dictator" (V, 57); the desire to be called "king" (V, 60). Instead, he gives us a man who wants "great Rome" to suck his "Reviving blood" (II.ii.87–88) and to take from it "tinctures, stains, relics, and cognizance" (89). This aspiration marks the difference between Caesar and the typical tyrant, who is himself blood-thirsty. Like the "man-eater" of Homer's famous description (*Iliad* I.231) and subsequent accounts, the typical tyrant devours others. In contrast, the vision of Caesar nourishing Rome with his blood borrows from Christian myth and ritual as well as from the stock political image of the king as fountain to characterize Caesar as a ruler just and good.

—Robert S. Miola, "*Julius Caesar* and the Tyrannicide Debate," *Renaissance Quarterly* 38, No. 2 (Summer 1985): 282–84

❖

[Paul N. Siegel (b. 1916) is a former professor of English at Long Island University in Brooklyn, New York. He has written voluminously on Shakespeare, including such books as *Shakespearean Tragedy and the Elizabethan Compromise* (1957) and *Shakespeare in His Time and Ours* (1968). In this extract from his Marxist interpretation of Shakespeare, Siegel maintains that Shakespeare and his Elizabethan contemporaries regarded the monarchical principle represented by Caesar as essential to the preservation of the state, so that his murder becomes a kind of natural catastrophe.]

To be sure, *Julius Caesar,* like *Richard II,* is not a simplistic propaganda tract. Many critics have found it to be enigmatic, being unsure with whom our sympathies are to lie. Not only does Brutus, a noble, kind person, join in the assassination of one who is his "best lover" (3.2.445), but Cassius, despite his envy of Caesar, has a genuinely deep affection for Brutus and is ruled by him against his better judgment. Most complex of all is Julius Caesar, who has accomplished remarkable feats, whose greatness and force of character are acknowledged by Brutus, who is loved by the common people, and who has generosity of spirit, as proved by his feeling for Brutus and Antony and by the fortune he leaves to the citizens of Rome, but who, carried away by ambition and intoxicated by his preeminence, is vainglorious, pompous, and boastful. Here Shakespeare, instead of welding together two disparate traditions, as in his depiction of Richard, draws upon a long-standing tradition of Caesar as a man in whom good and bad qualities were strongly intermixed. "In the literary treatment of Julius Caesar before Shakespeare," says Geoffrey Bullough, there was "a weighing of pros and cons, a representation of good and bad characteristics. . . . The English [Renaissance] attitude to Julius Caesar preserved its medieval ambivalence."

Yet, as in the case of *Richard II,* the play's language, imagery, and course of action indicate clearly enough how the fall of its title character should be regarded: Caesar is representative of the monarchical principle necessary for the well-being of Rome. Just before Caesar's assassination there are earthquakes, fearful storms, and other prodigies, as at the murder of Duncan, the "civil strife in heaven" (1.3.11) prefiguring the civil wars to come on earth. Brutus is "with himself at war" (1.2.46), his "little kingdom" suffering in itself "an insurrection" (2.1.68, 69), as Macbeth in doing what is unnatural has to fight against himself. The disagreement between the conspirators (2.1.101–11), like the disagreement between Glendower and Hotspur in *Henry IV, Part 1,* indicates the lack of unity and the discord to follow among the perpetrators of disorder. The disease imagery used in reference to Brutus and Caius Ligarius (2.1.235–68, 310–24) suggests the sickness of the enterprise, as does the sickness of Northumberland in *Henry IV, Part 1.* Caesar's invitation to the conspirators to "taste some wine with me" and then, "like friends" (2.2.126–27), go with him to the Senate House brings home that they, like Timon's friends at his banquet and Macbeth at the banquet for Duncan, are violating the communion of fellowship.

The panic of the people on hearing of the assassination, responding to the news "as it were doomsday" (3.1.98), is reminiscent of the doomsday imagery betokening the horrors of the deaths of Duncan and Lear. The ritual bathing of the conspirators in the blood of Caesar at the suggestion of Brutus, who would have it that they are "sacrificers," not "butchers" (2.1.166), is dramatically ironic: the "lofty scene" that Cassius prophesies "shall be acted over/ In states unborn and accents yet unknown" (3.1.112–13) was at the very moment being reenacted in English before an audience aware that this ceremony was really the "savage spectacle" (3.1.223) Brutus denied it to be and would inaugurate the savage butchery of civil war.

Antony's soliloquy prophesying this "domestic fury and fierce civil strife" (3.1.263) is, as Brents Stirling says, "similar in utterance, function, and dramatic placement to Carlisle's prophecy on the deposition of Richard II, and for that reason it is to be taken seriously as a choric interpretation of Caesar's death." Indeed the action that follows fulfills this prophecy that "Caesar's spirit, ranging for revenge," will, "with a monarch's voice / Cry havoc and let slip the dogs of war" (3.1.270–73).

The triumphant spirit of Caesar is really the principle of Caesarism, reincarnated in Octavius Caesar, the man of destiny who is to win out over his fellow triumvirs and establish the empire that will bring peace to all the known world.

—Paul N. Siegel, *Shakespeare's English and Roman History Plays: A Marxist Approach* (Rutherford, NJ: Fairleigh Dickinson University Press, 1986), pp. 97–98

❖

WAYNE A. REBHORN AND THE CRISIS OF THE ARISTOCRACY IN *JULIUS CAESAR*

[Wayne A. Rebhorn (b. 1943) is a professor of English at the University of Texas and the author of *Foxes and Lions: Machiavelli's Confidence Men* (1988) and *The Emperor of Men's Minds: Literature and the Renaissance Discourse of Rhetoric* (1955). In this extract, Rebhorn studies *Julius Caesar* in the context of Lawrence Stone's celebrated historical study, *The Crisis of the Aristocracy 1558–1641* (1967), in which Stone maintained that during this period the English aristocracy changed from a class of independent feudal magnates to obsequious courtiers increasingly dependent upon courtly favor.]

What I wish to argue about *Julius Caesar* is that the play uses Roman history in order to hold a mirror up to the state of Shakespeare's England, and in particular, to reflect and reflect on, to identify and provide terms for imagining, what Stone has called the crisis of the aristocracy. Like Stone, the play suggests that the aristocracy is undergoing a profound change that will eventuate in its ultimate loss as a class of any real power and influence, in its marginalization by increasingly absolutist monarchs who actually saw themselves reflected in the Roman emperors who came to power when Octavius finally triumphed and ended the civil wars whose initial stages *Julius Caesar* depicts. To be sure, the analytical perspective offered by the play is not Stone's: where the latter emphasizes economics and social history, the former presents the situation in moral terms.

Shakespeare's play is analytical, revealing the self-destruction, the suicide, to which an entire class is being impelled by its essential values and mode of self-definition, by its emulation and factionalism.

Like Stone, but in a far less casual manner, *Julius Caesar* characterizes the aristocracy and the state they inhabit as being sick, from the opening scene with its cobbler's jokes about being a "surgeon to old shoes" (I.1.23–24), through the epilepsy of Caesar, the physical ailment of Caius Ligarius, and the internal insurrection of Brutus that has made him unwell, down to the assassination itself that is imagined as making "whole" men "sick" (II.1.328). The crucial difference between Shakespeare's play and Stone on this score, however, is that the metaphors of *Julius Caesar* define the moral condition of a society going through an enormous change, identifying that change itself as illness, while Stone's metaphor of crisis is a rhetorical ploy, merely a conceptual instrument used to give shape to the history of the period. Moreover, the play does not benefit from Stone's hindsight. It presents the aristocracy on the way down, in the throes of a moral and social sickness from which it holds out no real hope of a recovery. Aristocratic emulation spells factionalism and civil strife, and it leads inevitably, tragically, to the dead-end of suicide. Lacking the advantage of Stone's longer view, *Julius Caesar* depicts a sick world in the process of succumbing to centralized, absolutist, one-man rule not because of the exceptional talents of characters such as Caesar and Octavius, but because of the emulation, the imperial will, which animates the behavior of the entire class of aristocrats and leads ineluctably to their unintended, collective self-destruction. Driven by the hunger of emulation to extend endlessly the terrain of the self, they destroy and will keep destroying one another until the stage is bare and only a single imperial will is left. As a character in another play, a play also concerned with emulation and factionalism, sums it up with fitting finality: the appetite driving them on is "an universal wolf"; it will "make perforce an universal prey / And last eat up himself" (*Troilus and Cressida*, I.3.121, 123–24).

—Wayne A. Rebhorn, "The Crisis of the Aristocracy in *Julius Caesar*," *Renaissance Quarterly* 43, No. 1 (Spring 1990): 108–9

❖

[René Girard (b. 1923), Andrew P. Hammond Professor of French at Stanford University, is the author of many important works of criticism and critical theory, including *Deceit, Desire, and the Novel* (1977), *Violence and the Sacred* (1977), and *A Theater of Envy: William Shakespeare* (1991). In this extract, Girard draws upon his earlier study, *The Scapegoat* (1986), in portraying Caesar as a sacrificial victim.]

Everything that Caesar does, everything that we learn about him as a public or a private individual, including the sterility of his wife—which the popular mind readily attributes to a husband's evil eye—make him look like a man earmarked for victimization. At one point he offers his throat to the crowd in a gesture reminiscent of some sacred king volunteering for the role of sacrificial victim. It is also significant that Caesar would be associated with both the Lupercalia and the Ides of March, two Roman festivals rooted, as all such festivals are, in so-called scapegoat rituals.

It may be objected that much of this is already in Plutarch; Shakespeare is simply repeating his source. He is closer to Plutarch, no doubt, than many critics are willing to admit, for fear, perhaps, of minimizing his originality. This fear is unfounded. Shakespeare's genius manifests itself first and foremost in his mimetic reading of Plutarch.

Plutarch's Caesar has all the telltale signs except for the bad ear. Even if this infirmity is not Shakespeare's own invention, even if this feature too comes from an ancient source, this additional scapegoat sign is significant. A lesser writer might have discarded all such signs as demeaning, unworthy of a great hero, uselessly superstitious. In "classical" France the bad ear and the falling sickness would have been condemned in the name of "good taste." For showing Attila dying of a nosebleed, the old Corneille was endlessly ridiculed. Being under no such pressure, Shakespeare carefully reproduced everything he found in Plutarch, and added a little more on his own.

When they talk about Caesar, Cassius and Casca constantly resort to such words as "monster" and "monstrous" in such an ambiguous way that all distinction between the physical and the moral is abolished. This practice encourages the victimization of physically abnormal people. When the world seems monstrous, such men as Casca seek some human embodiment of this monstrousness. They spurn rational explanations in favor of such magical formulas as "the man most like this dreadful night." Had he lived during the great medieval plagues, Casca would have persecuted Jews, lepers, and physically handicapped people. There were still witch-hunters in Shakespeare's world, and Casca and even Cassius are patterned after them.

In spite of his repudiation of astrology, Cassius is not really immune to the irrational influence of typical scapegoat features; his story of swimming across the Tiber reveals an obsessive concern with Caesar's physical infirmities. To Casca and even to Cassius, then, Caesar is certainly a scapegoat; is he one for Brutus as well? If one conspirator only can be regarded as rational, Brutus must be the one. His fascination with Caesar has nothing to do with epilepsy or the bad weather. Brutus may be excessively ambitious but his attachment to the Republic is sincere. He is obsessively jealous but his jealousy is really his own—authentic mimetic desire, so to speak, rather than a copy of a copy, as in the case of Casca.

Traditional criticism has always dealt with *Julius Caesar* as if Shakespeare happened to be a nineteenth-century historian writing from the standpoint of post-Enlightenment rationalism. The murderous political game of the play is treated as a perfectly rational activity. In order to challenge this reading, one must show that not even for Brutus is Caesar a rational target of assassination. If the scapegoat reading of the murder is applicable only to marginal characters such as Casca, its relevance is marginal as well, and there is a rational core to this play that my mimetic interpretation cannot touch.

This objection is already countered by the role played by mimesis in Brutus's decision to join the conspiracy, but the question is so crucial that the point must be further emphasized. As far as Brutus is concerned, it is true that Caesar is no borrowed rival, but he is borrowed *as a target of assassination*. This is what the scenes with Cassius make clear, and the point is confirmed by Brutus's soliloquy; he lost his sleep only after

Cassius "first did whet [him] against Caesar." Thoughts of murder did not enter his honest and virtuous soul spontaneously.

Even in Brutus's case, Caesar is a scapegoat. To clinch this fundamental point, Shakespeare makes Brutus's political indictment of Caesar extremely weak and unconvincing. Brutus honestly acknowledges that Caesar has not yet abused his power; he does not deserve to die (II, i).

What matters here is not the historical accuracy of this interpretation (the play makes no allusion to Caesar's illegal crossing of the Rubicon), but its implications for the type of victim that Shakespeare wants Caesar to be. He wants his murder to be unjustifiable, even from an extreme republican standpoint. His reason for denying the essential rationality of the murder is not his personal preference for Caesar or for the monarchical principle, but his overall mimetic view of human relations, the whole basis for his conception of tragedy.

How could Caesar fail to be a scapegoat anyway, since his murderers want him to be responsible for a whole crisis of Degree? Such a crisis can only be regarded as the responsibility of all citizens, or of none at all, since its roots go far back into the past—to the very beginning, as a matter of fact. In no case can this crisis be the responsibility of a single individual, however powerful he happens to be. Brutus's reasoning is a less fantastic version of "the man most like this dreadful night," a political rather than a magicocosmological version. Ultimately all murderers are equally irrational and undifferentiated.

—René Girard, "Great Rome Shall Suck Reviving Blood: The Founding Murder in *Julius Caesar*," *A Theater of Envy: William Shakespeare* (New York: Oxford University Press, 1991), pp. 205–7

❖

VIVIAN THOMAS ON THE GENRE OF *JULIUS CAESAR*

[Vivian Thomas is the author of *The Moral Universe of Shakespeare's Problem Plays* (1987) and *Shakespeare's*

Roman Worlds (1989). In this extract, Thomas studies the complex issue of the genre classification of *Julius Caesar*, finding it simultaneously a revenge tragedy and a Roman play.]

What emerges from the briefest glance at some of the most significant contributions to the discussion of genre and the unity of the play is that unless it is seen simply as a revenge tragedy it constitutes a pathbreaking drama which differs quite markedly from the English histories that precede it and the tragedies which come later. Whereas in *Titus Andronicus* Shakespeare conveys a genuine sense of a Roman world, the play itself looks in two directions: towards the later Roman plays and towards *King Lear*. With *Julius Caesar,* Shakespeare comes face to face with Rome for the second time in his dramatic career, but is influenced for the first time by Plutarch. Here he creates a truly palpable sense of Rome with its great historical figures populating the social and physical landscape, speaking in a distinctive manner, and struggling with tensions arising from those most deep-rooted of human emotions— love, jealousy and ambition—while trying to live up to the conception of a true Roman. Entering the theatre we are drawn into a political maelstrom. We are never allowed to forget the nature of political conflict and even in the final moments there is an acute consciousness of an embryonic conflict between Antony and Octavius with the latter stealing the initiative. As Brutus makes his confident prediction about the verdict of history, the audience is provoked into a contemplation of the historical events and interpretations. There is also an attempt to assess personal and political motives, decisions and consequences—matters quite absent at the end of a tragedy.

If the question of genre had troubled the minds of Shakespeare's audience, they would probably have felt that it was a Roman play and that it was a tragedy. Its strain of revenge tragedy would almost certainly have struck a chord. But it is doubtful whether they would have been troubled further. Perhaps the foremost question in their minds on leaving the theatre would have been 'who was right?'—a question which many might have expected to have been answered. What they experienced was something opaque. For subsequent audiences justification of the assassination would be determined, largely, by the proclivity of the production or the nature of the social world outside the theatre. If Julius Caesar is identified with fascist dictators, sympathy for Brutus is strong. If the proscription scene is cut and a charismatic actor plays Antony, he can emerge as the hero. How the play is received will depend greatly on the weighting of the major protagonists and/or by a variety of directorial decisions, because it is not possible to make unequivocal statements based on the text. Moreover, even in the case of a most carefully balanced production working with an uncut text, reaction will inevitably be influenced by personal and political prejudices.

Shakespeare presents us with an enigma in such a way as to make unequivocal judgement impossible. We cannot even be certain about the kind of play it is, other than by calling it a Roman play. It is almost half a century since John Palmer drew attention to a crucial unifying feature, that ubiquitous Roman character, the Roman crowd, present from the outset and playing a vital part in the determination of events. The very Romanness of *Julius Caesar* provides its chief unifying element. There is no doubt that the latter part of the play can seem sprawling or anticlimactic, but it is also possible to sustain the dramatic tension right up to the final curtain—and beyond. As the final battle ends the embryo of a future struggle emerges in the exchanges between the vividly contrasting personalities of Antony and Octavius. Already the Roman world is experiencing a process of metamorphosis. Concern is not just with the dead, but with the living, and with the process of history itself, and how that strange feeling of historical inevitability works its spell on all observers, even after we have watched, in minute detail, the interplay between personalities, values, decisions and events. The unity of the play resides in its living, pulsating Roman world and in its stimulation of that insatiable human curiosity about history—and how it might have been.

—Vivian Thomas, *Julius Caesar* (New York: Twayne, 1992), pp. 22–24

❖

Books by
William Shakespeare

Venus and Adonis. 1593.

The Rape of Lucrece. 1594.

Henry VI. 1594.

Titus Andronicus. 1594.

The Taming of the Shrew. 1594.

Romeo and Juliet. 1597.

Richard III. 1597.

Richard II. 1597.

Love's Labour's Lost. 1598.

Henry IV. 1598.

The Passionate Pilgrim. 1599.

A Midsummer Night's Dream. 1600.

The Merchant of Venice. 1600.

Much Ado about Nothing. 1600.

Henry V. 1600.

The Phoenix and the Turtle. 1601.

The Merry Wives of Windsor. 1602.

Hamlet. 1603.

King Lear. 1608.

Troilus and Cressida. 1609.

Sonnets. 1609.

Pericles. 1609.

Othello. 1622.

Mr. William Shakespeares Comedies, Histories & Tragedies. Ed. John Heminge and Henry Condell. 1623 (First Folio), 1632 (Second Folio), 1663 (Third Folio), 1685 (Fourth Folio).

Poems. 1640.

Works. Ed. Nicholas Rowe. 1709. 6 vols.

Works. Ed. Alexander Pope. 1723–25. 6 vols.

Works. Ed. Lewis Theobald. 1733. 7 vols.

Works. Ed. Thomas Hanmer. 1743–44. 6 vols.

Works. Ed. William Warburton. 1747. 8 vols.

Plays. Ed. Samuel Johnson. 1765. 8 vols.

Plays and Poems. Ed. Edmond Malone. 1790. 10 vols.

The Family Shakespeare. Ed. Thomas Bowdler. 1807. 4 vols.

Works. Ed. J. Payne Collier. 1842–44. 8 vols.

Works. Ed. H. N. Hudson. 1851–56. 11 vols.

Works. Ed. Alexander Dyce. 1857. 6 vols.

Works. Ed. Richard Grant White. 1857–66. 12 vols.

Works (Cambridge Edition). Ed. William George Clark, John Glover, and William Aldis Wright. 1863–66. 9 vols.

A New Variorum Edition of the Works of Shakespeare. Ed. H. H. Furness et al. 1871– .

Works. Ed. W. J. Rolfe. 1871–96. 40 vols.

The Pitt Press Shakespeare. Ed. A. W. Verity. 1890–1905. 13 vols.

The Warwick Shakespeare. 1893–1938. 13 vols.

The Temple Shakespeare. Ed. Israel Gollancz. 1894–97. 40 vols.

The Arden Shakespeare. Ed. W. J. Craig, R. H. Case et al. 1899–1924. 37 vols.

The Shakespeare Apocrypha. Ed. C. F. Tucker Brooke. 1908.

The Yale Shakespeare. Ed. Wilbur L. Cross, Tucker Brooke, and Willard Highley Durham. 1917–27. 40 vols.

The New Shakespeare (Cambridge Edition). Ed. Arthur Quiller-Couch and John Dover Wilson. 1921–62. 38 vols.

The New Temple Shakespeare. Ed. M. R. Ridley. 1934–36. 39 vols.

Works. Ed. George Lyman Kittredge. 1936.

The Penguin Shakespeare. Ed. G. B. Harrison. 1937–59. 36 vols.

The New Clarendon Shakespeare. Ed. R. E. C. Houghton. 1938– .

The Arden Shakespeare. Ed. Una Ellis-Fermor et al. 1951– .

The Complete Pelican Shakespeare. Ed. Alfred Harbage. 1969.

The Complete Signet Classic Shakespeare. Ed. Sylvan Barnet. 1972.

The Oxford Shakespeare. Ed. Stanley Wells. 1982– .

The New Cambridge Shakespeare. Ed. Philip Brockbank. 1984– .

Works about
William Shakespeare and
Julius Caesar

Anderson, Peter S. "Shakespeare's *Caesar:* The Language of Sacrifice." *Comparative Drama* 3 (1969–70): 3–26.

Anson, John. "Julius Caesar: The Politics of the Hardened Heart." *Shakespeare Studies* 2 (1966): 11–33.

Barton, Anne. "*Julius Caesar* and *Coriolanus:* Shakespeare's Roman World of Words." In *Shakespeare's Craft,* ed. Philip H. Highfill, Jr. Carbondale: George Washington University/Southern Illinois University Press, 1982, pp. 24–47.

Berry, Ralph. "Communal Identity and the Rituals of *Julius Caesar.*" In Berry's *Shakespeare and the Awareness of the Audience.* London: Macmillan, 1985, pp. 75–89.

Blits, Jan H. *The End of the Ancient Republic: Essays on* Julius Caesar. Durham: Carolina Academic Press, 1982.

Bloom, Harold, ed. *Julius Caesar.* New York: Chelsea House, 1994.

———, ed. *William Shakespeare's* Julius Caesar. New York: Chelsea House, 1988.

Bulman, James C. *The Heroic Idiom of Shakespearean Tragedy.* Newark: University of Delaware Press, 1985.

Charney, Maurice. "The Imagery of *Julius Caesar.*" In Charney's *Shakespeare's Roman Plays: The Function of Imagery in the Drama.* Cambridge, MA: Harvard University Press, 1961, pp. 41–78.

Danson, Lawrence. *Tragic Alphabet: Shakespeare's Drama of Language.* New Haven: Yale University Press, 1974.

Eagleton, Terry. *Shakespeare and Society: Critical Studies in Shakespearean Drama.* New York: Schocken Books, 1967.

Edinborough, Arnold. *"Julius Caesar."* In *Manner and Meaning in Shakespeare,* ed. B. A. W. Jackson. Dublin: McMaster University Library Press/Irish University Press, 1969, pp. 129–44.

Furtwangler, Albert. *Assassin on Stage: Brutus, Hamlet, and the Death of Lincoln.* Urbana: University of Illinois Press, 1991.

Ghose, Zulfikar. *Shakespeare's Mortal Knowledge: A Reading of the Tragedies.* Basingstoke, UK: Macmillan Press, 1993.

Goldman, Michael. *Acting and Action in Shakespearean Tragedy.* Princeton: Princeton University Press, 1985.

Greene, Gayle. " 'The Power of Speech / To Stir Men's Blood': The Language of Tragedy in Shakespeare's *Julius Caesar."* *Renaissance Drama* 11 (1980): 67–93.

Grene, Nicholas. *Shakespeare's Tragic Imagination.* New York: St. Martin's Press, 1992.

Harrison, G. B. *Shakespeare's Tragedies.* London: Routledge & Kegan Paul, 1951.

———, ed. *Julius Caesar in Shakespeare, Shaw, and the Ancients.* New York: Harcourt, Brace, 1960.

Hobson, Alan. *Full Circle: Shakespeare and Moral Development.* London: Chatto & Windus, 1972.

Holland, Norman N. *The Shakespearean Imagination.* New York: Macmillan, 1964.

Holloway, John. *The Story of the Night: Studies in Shakespeare's Major Tragedies.* London: Routledge & Kegan Paul, 1961.

Jones, Emrys. *Scenic Form in Shakespeare.* Oxford: Clarendon Press, 1971.

Kayser, John R., and Ronald J. Lettieri. " 'The Last of All the Romans': Shakespeare's Commentary on Classical Republicanism." *Clio* 9 (1979–80): 197–227.

Knight, G. Wilson. *Shakespeare's Dramatic Challenge: On the Rise of Shakespeare's Tragic Heroes.* London: Croom Helm; New York: Barnes & Noble, 1977.

Knights, L. C. "Personality and Politics in *Julius Caesar.*" In Knights's *Further Explorations.* Stanford: Stanford University Press, 1965, pp. 33–52.

Leggatt, Alexander. *Shakespeare's Political Drama: The History Plays and the Roman Plays.* London: Routledge, 1988.

Liebler, Naomi Conn. " 'Thou Bleeding Piece of Earth': The Ritual Ground of *Julius Caesar.*" *Shakespeare Studies* 14 (1981): 175–96.

McAlindon, T. *Shakespeare and Decorum.* London: Macmillan, 1973.

————. *Shakespeare's Tragic Cosmos.* Cambridge: Cambridge University Press, 1991.

Mangan, Michael. *A Preface to Shakespeare's Tragedies.* London: Longman, 1991.

Margolies, David. *Monsters of the Deep: Social Dissolution in Shakespeare's Tragedies.* Manchester, UK: Manchester University Press, 1992.

Morris, Ivor. *Shakespeare's God: The Role of Religion in the Tragedies.* London: George Allen & Unwin, 1972.

Nevo, Ruth. *Tragic Form in Shakespeare.* Princeton: Princeton University Press, 1972.

Paster, Gail Kern. " 'In the Spirit of Men There Is No Blood': Blood as Trope of Gender in *Julius Caesar.*" *Shakespeare Quarterly* 40 (1989): 284–98.

Prior, Moody E. "The Search for a Hero in *Julius Caesar.*" *Renaissance Drama* 2 (1969): 81–101.

Prosner, Matthew N. *The Heroic Image in Five Shakespearean Tragedies.* Princeton: Princeton University Press, 1965.

Rabkin, Norman. "Structure, Convention, and Meaning in *Julius Caesar.*" *Journal of English and Germanic Philology* 63 (1964): 240–54.

Ribner, Irving. *Patterns in Shakespearian Tragedy.* London: Methuen, 1960.

Ripley, John. Julius Caesar *on Stage in England and America, 1599–1973.* Cambridge: Cambridge University Press, 1980.

Rose, Mark. "Conjuring Caesar: Ceremony, History, and Authority in 1599." *English Literary Renaissance* 19 (1989): 291–304.

Rosen, William. *Shakespeare and the Craft of Tragedy.* Cambridge, MA: Harvard University Press, 1960.

Ryan, Kiernan. *Shakespeare.* Atlantic Highlands, NJ: Humanities Press, 1989.

Schanzer, Ernest. *The Problem Plays of Shakespeare.* New York: Schocken Books, 1963.

Schwartz, Elias. *The Mortal Worm: Shakespeare's Master Theme.* Port Washington, NY: Kennikat Press, 1977.

Siemon, James R. *Shakespearean Iconoclasm.* Berkeley: University of California Press, 1985.

Smith, Molly. *The Darker World Within: Evil in the Tragedies of Shakespeare and His Successors.* Newark: University of Delaware Press, 1991.

Stampfer, Judah. *The Tragic Engagement: A Study of Shakespeare's Classical Tragedies.* New York: Funk & Wagnalls, 1968.

Taylor, Myron. "Shakespeare's *Julius Caesar* and the Irony of History." *Shakespeare Quarterly* 24 (1973): 301–8.

Thomas, Vivian. *Shakespeare's Roman Worlds.* London: Routledge, 1989.

Traversi, Derek. *Shakespeare: The Roman Plays.* Stanford: Stanford University Press, 1963.

Velz, John W. "Clemency, Will, and Just Cause in *Julius Caesar.*" *Shakespeare Survey* 22 (1969): 109–18.

Wilson, Richard. " 'Is This a Holiday?' Shakespeare's Roman Carnival." *ELH* 54 (1987): 31–44.

———. *William Shakespeare, Julius Caesar.* London: Penguin, 1992.

Yoder, R. A. "History and the Histories in *Julius Caesar.*" *Shakespeare Quarterly* 24 (1973): 309–27.

Index of
Themes and Ideas